# Breastfeeding: Laws and Societal Impact

# BREASTFEEDING: LAWS AND SOCIETAL IMPACT

SARAH W. YING
EDITOR

Nova Science Publishers, Inc.
*New York*

For permission to use material from this book please contact us:
Telephone 631-231-7269; Fax 631-231-8175
Web Site: http://www.novapublishers.com



LIBRARY OF CONGRESS CATALOGING-IN-PUBLICATION DATA

Breastfeeding: Laws and Societal Impact/ Sarah W. Ying, editor.
p. cm.
Includes index.
ISBN 1-59454-754-8 (hardcover)
1. Breastfeeding: Laws and Societal Impact. I. Ying, Sarah W.
QC173.7.T74 2004
530.14'072--dc22 2004024758

Published by Nova Science Publishers, Inc. ✢New York

# CONTENTS

# PREFACE

The rate of breastfeeding in the United States has risen and fallen over time as a result of changing lifestyles and the availability of substitutes for human milk. However, since the 1970s the rates of breastfeeding initiation and duration have increased, in part due to the increasing medical evidence of the significant health benefits both to mothers and children. The federal government's Health Objectives for 2010 are for 75% of mothers to initiate breastfeeding at the time of birth and for 50% to continue breastfeeding until their infants reach 6 months of age. Current rates are about 69.5% at the time of hospital discharge and 32.5% at 6 months of age. The health benefits to the infant include the high nutritional quality of human milk, and a decrease in various infectious and other diseases of infancy that are reduced by the anti-microbial, anti-inflammatory and immunological-stimulating agents present. Mothers seem to benefit with a more rapid return to the pre-pregnancy state of their bodies, improved glucose and lipid metabolism, delayed ovulation, and the possible reduction of certain cancers. This new book examines the impact on health, employment and society, laws and government support of this important health action.

In: Breastfeeding: Laws and Societal Impact ISBN 1-59454-754-8
Editor: Sarah W. Ying, pp. 1-13 

*Chapter 1*

# Breast-Feeding: Impact on Health, Employment and Society*

***Donna V. Porter***

## Summary

The rate of breast-feeding in the United States has risen and fallen over time as a result of changing lifestyles and the availability of substitutes for human milk. However, since the 1970s the rates of breast-feeding initiation and duration have increased, in part due to the increasing medical evidence of the significant health benefits both to mothers and children. The federal government's Health Objectives for 2010 are for 75% of mothers to initiate breast-feeding at the time of birth and for 50% to continue breast-feeding until their infants reach 6 months of age. Current rates are about 69.5% at the time of hospital discharge and 32.5% at 6 months of age.

The health benefits to the infant include the high nutritional quality of human milk, and a decrease in various infectious and other diseases of infancy that are reduced by the anti-microbial, anti-inflammatory and immunological-stimulating agents present. Mothers seem to benefit with a more rapid return to the prepregnancy state of their bodies, improved glucose and lipid

* Excerpted from CRS Report RL32002, dated July 18, 2003.

metabolism, delayed ovulation, and the possible reduction of certain cancers.

Proponents of workplace lactation programs cite their benefits to employers as reduced employee absenteeism, increased productivity, increased company loyalty and morale, lower health care costs, and improved employee retention. The societal benefits of increased breast-feeding may include significant savings in health care costs, savings in the costs of infant formula, and the potential that intellectual development of children is enhanced by breast-feeding in the first year of life.

Breast-feeding promotion is a policy promoted by the U.S. Government and numerous non-governmental organizations. The infant formula industry also publishes educational literature that promotes breast-feeding as the preferred method of infant feeding in the first year of life.

Federal legislation has promoted various aspects of breast-feeding. The Treasury and General Government Appropriations Acts of the last 4 years have contained a provision that supports breast-feeding at government sites. In the 108th Congress, the Pregnancy Discrimination Act Amendments of 2003 (S. 418) was introduced to protect the rights of new mothers to breast-feed. Language in the Leave No Child Behind Act of 2003 (H.R. 936 and S. 448) would require consideration of government policies to provide lactation facilities, support and services in the federal government; it was reintroduced from the 107th Congress. The Breastfeeding Promotion Act (H.R. 285), introduced in the 107th Congress, would have provided protection of breast-feeding by new mothers, required development of a performance standard for breast pumps, and provided tax incentives to encourage employers to provide lactation programs. As of November 2002, 32 States had enacted legislation to protect mothers and promote breast-feeding.

This report will be updated to track legislative developments.

Women with infants and toddlers are a significant segment of the labor force today. As a result, a variety of laws and policies have been modified to provide the opportunity for these women to be successful both as parents and employees. This report summarizes information on the impact of breast-feeding on the health of mother and child, and on employers and employees where lactation support programs or other workplace supports are provided. Also addressed are current administrative and congressional efforts to promote breast-feeding.

## TRENDS IN BREAST-FEEDING AND LIFESTYLE

Until 1950, almost all U.S. babies were breast-fed, but in the last 50 years, infant feeding has changed dramatically.[1] Following World War II, bottle feeding became popular with the development and large-scale manufacture of infant formula products. Between 1946 and 1956, breast-feeding fell by 50%, and by 1967, only 25% of American infants were being breast-fed at the time of hospital discharge. By 1982 the percentage of breast-fed infants at discharge had grown to about 62%, declined to around 46% in 1990, and then had another upswing, reaching 64% in 1998.[2] The pattern of breast-feeding for 6 month old infants parallels that for newborns, although at a considerably lower rate. In 1998, about 29% of 6 month old infants were being breast-fed. Current U.S. rates of breast-feeding are 69.5% for mothers in-hospital and 32.5% at 6 months postpartum, despite recommendations from government and health professional organizations to breast-feed until at least 6 months of age.[3] The Healthy People 2010 targets, set by the federal government, are for 75% breast-feeding in-hospital and 50% breast-feeding at 6 months of age.

While the overall rates of breast-feeding have increased in recent years, the rates have remained uneven among various population groups.[4] Breast-feeding rates have generally been higher in western states, and among women who were older, college educated and multiparous (given birth several times), those who had not enrolled in the Special Supplemental Nutrition Program for Women, Infants and Children (WIC), were not employed outside the home, had normal birth weight infants and had higher disposable incomes. Recent increases have been greater among groups that have historically been less likely to practice breast-feeding: women who were black, younger than 25 years of age, in the lowest income group (less than $10,000 annually), have no more than a grade school education, primiparous (given birth once), lived in the south Atlantic region, had low birth weight infants, were employed full time outside the home, and participated in WIC. However, these groups still remain the least likely to initiate breast-feeding.

## HEALTH IMPACTS FOR MOTHERS AND INFANTS

The documented advantages of extended breast-feeding include nutritional, immunological and psychological benefits to both the mother and child. Human milk provides optimal nutrition to infants in both its composition and balance of nutrients. The relatively low protein content is adequate nutritionally, while not putting an unnecessary load of nitrogen on the immature kidney. Human milk protein is mainly whey, which is easily digestible by the infant. Generous amounts of essential fatty acids, saturated fatty acids, medium-chain triglycerides and cholesterol are also present. Long-chain polyunsaturated fatty acids promote optimal development of the central nervous system. Breast milk is relatively low in sodium content, allowing fluid requirements to be met without overwhelming the renal load. The minerals in human milk are protein-bound and balanced for bioavailability, and it provides iron, zinc, and calcium to meet infant needs, while putting a minimal demand on the maternal supply of these nutrients.

Recent recommendations from the American Academy of Pediatrics suggest that exclusively breast-fed infants should receive vitamin D supplementation to prevent rickets.[5] The Academy recommends that vitamin supplements begin at 2 months of age and continue until the infants are consuming at least 17 ounces daily of vitamin- D fortified milk. The use of multivitamins containing 200 international units of vitamin D is suggested, because supplements containing only vitamin D generally are too concentrated to be safe for routine use. The recommendation also applied to nonbreast-fed babies who are drinking less than17 ounces of fortified formula or milk daily, as well as children and adolescents who do not drink that much fortified milk, get regular sunlight exposure or take multiple vitamins with at least 200 international units of vitamin D. Previously, physicians believed that babies got adequate amounts of vitamin D, because sunlight stimulates the body to produce vitamin D. However, recent recognition that sunlight exposure over time is a risk factor for skin cancer has led to protecting children, and infants in particular, from direct sunlight, so they are not making the vitamin D that this exposure once provided. In recent years, there have been reports of dozens of cases of rickets nationwide, caused by a deficiency of vitamin D.

Human milk contains a variety of components that provide protection against common infectious diseases by inhibiting the growth of microbial pathogens, and enhance the nutritional status of infants under conditions in which poor sanitation and low quality weaning foods are present.[6] In addition, human milk contains an array of antimicrobial agents, anti-inflammatory agents, and immunologic stimulating agents, most of which are absent from or present in only small amounts in infant formula, and which the infant produces only in limited amounts. Research has demonstrated significant protection during breast-feeding against diarrhea, respiratory infections, otitis media, bacteremia, bacterial meningitis, botulism, urinary tract infections and necrotizing enterocolitis.[7] The frequency of gastrointestinal infections appears to be significantly lower in breast-fed infants compared to formula-fed infants. For some infections, the duration is shorter and the intensity is less in breast-fed infants than in formula-fed infants. In addition, breast milk appears to be protective against food allergies.

While considerable attention has focused on the health benefits of breast-feeding for the infant, which is the reason given by most women who choose to breast-feed, considerably less attention has been given to the health effects of breast-feeding on the mothers. A1991 National Academy of Sciences report concluded that there was insufficient evidence at that time to reach any conclusions on the impact of breastfeeding on maternal health, beyond the delay of return to regular ovulation.[8] A more recent review of the maternal health benefits examined the short- and long-term advantages from the available literature, which continues to be limited.[9] Breastfeeding in the early postpartum period was shown to promote a more rapid return of the uterus to its pre-pregnant state, and may also lead to a more rapid return to prepregnant weight. Among studies on duration and intensity of lactation, the majority showed a significant association between lactation and weight loss, although the researchers reported that there is no evidence that lactation prevents obesity. Lactation also seems to affect glucose and lipid metabolism, which may have implications for preventing the subsequent development of diabetes and heart disease. Lactation delays the return of ovulation and significantly reduces fertility during the period of lactational amenorrhea. While the researchers reported that the evidence from epidemiological studies is mixed, several large studies have shown that extended lactation is associated with reduced risk of premenopausal breast, ovarian and endometrial cancers. While bone mineralization declines during lactation, repletion occurs after weaning, and does not seem to cause long-term bone loss or increase the risk of osteoporosis.

A number of health and professional organizations have policies and positions supporting breast-feeding promotion, including the American Academy of Family Physicians, American Academy of Pediatrics, American Dietetic Association, American College of Nurse-Midwives, American College of Obstetricians and Gynecologists, Association of Women's Health, Obstetric and Neonatal Nurses, and National Association of Pediatric Nurse Practitioners. In addition, the infant formula industry, which consists of four companies in the United States, provides literature that supports the view that breast-feeding is the best choice in the first year of life. An example is the recent publication of Abbott Laboratories.[10]

## Societal Impact of Breast-Feeding Promotion

The recognized societal benefits of an increase in the rate of breast-feeding until infants are 6 months old include the savings that might be realized in health care costs. An analysis of the economic benefits of breast-feeding, conducted by the Economic Research Service of the U.S. Department of Agriculture and published in 2001, estimated that a minimum of $3.6 billion could be saved in the United States if breast-feeding increased from current levels to the levels recommended in Healthy People 2010.[11] This analysis represents cost savings from treatment of three childhood illnesses (otitis media, gastroenteritis, and necrotizing enterocolitis) and probably underestimates total savings, according to the researchers.

The savings to families of reduced spending on infant formula are substantial as well. Recent estimates are that out-of-pocket costs for families that use infant formula amount to $855 for the first 6 months of life.[12] While breast-feeding would likely result in some increase in food costs, since lactating women have increased nutrient needs, this cost would likely be less than the cost of infant formula for a year. The cost of purchasing formula has been shown to be several hundred dollars more than the cost of providing supplemental food for the breast-feeding mother.[13]

Finally, breast-feeding may enhance the intellectual development of children due to the benefits of certain polyunsaturated fatty acids (DHA — docosahexaenoic acid and AA — arachidonic acid) that have been demonstrated to promote visual and neural development. The recent decision by infant formula manufacturers to add these expensive fatty acids to their products in order to provide a product more comparable to human milk suggests recognition of the potential benefit of these ingredients, especially to premature infants.

## Factors Affecting the Decision to Breast-Feed

Decisions to initiate or refrain from breast-feeding are made for various reasons, but a number of barriers to breast-feeding have been identified. A significant factor is that breast-feeding is not necessarily accepted as a cultural norm, particularly within certain demographic groups. The decline in breast-feeding several decades ago led to a loss of traditional knowledge and support from the older generation for new mothers who wanted to breast-feed. In addition, health care professionals frequently lack adequate training in lactation and managing breast-feeding problems when they arise with new mothers. Societal changes in childbearing and child rearing, such as the increased numbers of teenage and single mothers and more reliance on child care outside the home, also create challenges to sustained breastfeeding. In the workplace, the relatively short term of maternity leave and difficulty of maintaining an adequate milk supply with prolonged separation from the infant contribute to early termination of breast-feeding. The effect of the commercial sector on breast-feeding has also had an impact through both marketing practices and the availability of products that promote the use of human milk substitutes, especially when these products are provided in hospital discharge packages.

While full-time work has been shown to have no effect on the initiation of breast-feeding, it does seem to have a profound effect on breast-feeding duration.[14] One survey found that while equal numbers of employed and unemployed mothers initiated breast-feeding, by the time their infants were 6 months old, only 10% of full-time employed working women reported that they were still breast-feeding, compared to 24% of non-employed women.[15] Women who are presumed to have the most influence over their working conditions, i.e., professional women, are the most likely to breast feed after returning to work and have the longest duration of breastfeeding, regardless of the length of maternity leave. The duration of maternity leave was shown to be highly significantly associated with the duration of breast-feeding. However, this association does not necessarily mean that returning to work directly causes weaning. Some women may wean in anticipation of returning to work, while others may wean in the face of difficulties in managing both work and breastfeeding. [16]

Breast-feeding supporters advocate a variety of ways to promote the initiation and duration of breast-feeding, including more part-time employment opportunities, improved training for health care personnel, longer maternity leaves, greater access to child care and lactation facilities in the workplace, and education campaigns to promote public recognition that breast-feeding for at least 6 months is optimal, with the use of human milk substitutes reserved only for a minority of infants with specific indications. There are situations in which breast-feeding is not generally possible or appropriate, such as in mothers who are HIV-positive, use illegal drugs, are receiving chemotherapy, have physical or mental disabilities that prevent effective or adequate milk production, or in cases of adoption or multiple births. Some women simply choose not to breast-feed.

Given the number of women of childbearing age currently in the workforce, the provision of lactation support for those mothers who wish to breast-feed after returning to work has been advocated as an employment benefit that could serve as an incentive to select or remain in a job. Providing easily accessible and comfortable surroundings for women to use breast pumps to express milk and/or day care so that babies can be fed on-site is seen as a way to support a woman's desire to breast-feed. In making a decision to provide lactation support facilities, factors considered by employers include such issues as company size and the type of work a company or agency performed that will be interrupted when breast-feeding occurs. Workplace lactation programs have been suggested to provide a relatively inexpensive way to reduce employee absenteeism, increase productivity, increase company loyalty and morale, lower health care costs and improve employee retention.[17] The provision of lactation services at the work site and during maternity leave seem to both enhance a woman's ability to initiate and sustain breast-feeding her child as well as commitment to the employer.

One review of the rise in breast-feeding in the United States suggested that pressure to remove existing barriers to breast-feeding could eventually come from health maintenance organizations and insurance companies, which are increasingly likely to recognize the costs of not breast-feeding. The author identified such options as flexible work hours and paid maternity leave, offered either by the government or family-friendly workplaces, that could increase the ability of employed women to optimally feed their infants.[18] In countries where governments have passed laws which guarantee all mothers paid leave from their work (with as much as 80% of their salary) for 9 months after childbirth (and in some cases up to a year), there has been a significant increase in the prevalence of breast-feeding between 6 and 9 months of age.[19] The World Health Organization/UNICEF program to create "babyfriendly" maternity hospitals, with the goal of enabling all women to practice exclusive breast-feeding immediately after birth, is credited with further supporting the increase in breast-feeding in countries where this program has been implemented.[20]

# Government Policies to Promote Breast-Feeding

In 2000 the Department of Health and Human Services (HHS) under the auspices of Surgeon General of the United States issued its HHS Blueprint for Action on Breastfeeding.[21] The document outlined the public health challenge of breastfeeding, the benefits of and cautions about breast-feeding, facilitations and support for breast-feeding, major HHS breast-feeding activities in the 1990s and the blueprint for action on breast-feeding. The intent of this report was to provide a comprehensive framework under which a variety of governmental programs and policies would be pursued to increase breast-feeding and promote breast-feeding practices.

In 1998, the U.S. Breastfeeding Committee was established to develop a strategic plan to protect, promote and support breast-feeding in the United States. The committee is supported by the HHS Health Resources and Services Administration's Maternal and Child Health Bureau. It is composed of representatives from over three dozen health professional organizations and relevant government departments and non-governmental organizations. The committee's strategic plan, published in 2001, has four goals, which have related objectives and strategies to achieve them.

- assure access to comprehensive, current and culturally appropriate lactation care and services for all women, children and families;
- ensure that breast-feeding is recognized as the normal and preferred method of feeding infants and young children;
- ensure that all federal, state and local laws relating to child welfare and family law recognize and support the importance and practice of breast-feeding; and
- increase protection, promotion and support for breast-feeding mothers in the workforce.

# Congressional Action on Breast-Feeding Promotion

In the last two decades, numerous bills have been introduced in Congress that addressed various aspects of breast-feeding promotion. Many bills addressed breastfeeding in the context of the Special Supplemental

Nutrition Program for Women, Infants and Children (WIC), which will not be discussed in this report. (See CRS Report RL31577, *Child Nutrition and WIC Programs: Background and Funding.*)

The Treasury and General Government Appropriations Acts of 2000, 2001, 2002, and 2003 (P.L. 106-58, P.L. 106-554, P.L. 107-67, and P.L. 108-7) were each enacted with a provision that supports breast-feeding at government sites. The identical language in these Acts states that "notwithstanding any other provision of law, a woman may breast-feed her child at any location in a federal building or on federal property, if the woman and her child are otherwise authorized to be present at the location." This provision supports breast-feeding by both federal employees and visitors.

The Pregnancy Discrimination Act Amendments of 2003, S. 418, has been introduced by Senator Snowe in the 108th Congress. This bill would protect the rights of new mothers to breast-feed their infants, by amending the Civil Rights Act of 1964 to include lactation, including the expression of milk, within the definitions of "because of sex" or "on the basis of sex" for purposes of the Act. It was referred to the Committee on Health, Education, Labor and Pensions, but no further action has been taken. The bill was also introduced in the 107th Congress.

Identical bills, introduced in the 108th Congress as the Leave No Child Behind Act of 2003 (H.R. 936 and S. 448), by Representative G. Miller and Senator Dodd respectively, contain a provision that provides for an interagency council to be established by the administrator of the General Services Administration. This council would address policy issues regarding child care, including the provision of areas for nursing mothers and other lactation support facilities and services, in the federal government. Similar legislation was introduced in the 107th Congress, but no action was taken on H.R. 1990 and S. 940.

A bill, entitled the Breastfeeding Promotion Act, H.R. 285, was introduced in the 107th Congress by Representative Maloney. Title I, to be known as the Pregnancy Discrimination Act Amendments of 2001, would have amended the Civil Rights Act of 1964 as described above in relation to S. 418. Title II would have provided a tax credit for employer expenses providing an appropriate environment on the business' premises for employed mothers to breast-feed or express milk for their children, by amending the Internal Revenue Code to allow a limited credit to employers for expenses incurred in enabling employed mothers to breast-feed. Title III, the Safe and Effective Breast Pump Act, directed the Secretary of HHS to establish and implement a performance standard for breast pumps irrespective of the classification of the breast pumps under the Federal Food, Drug and Cosmetic Act, and to issue a compliance policy guide which would ensure that women who want to breast-feed a child are given full and complete information regarding breast pumps. Title IV would have expanded the Internal Revenue Code definition of medical care to include qualified breast-feeding equipment and services. The bill was referred to the Committees on Ways and Means, Education and the Workforce, and Energy and Commerce. No further action was taken by any committee.

## State Breast-Feeding Statutes

As of November 2002, 32 states had enacted legislation related to breastfeeding. Seventeen states permit mothers to breast-feed in any public or private location where the mother is legally entitled to do so. Thirteen states have exempted breast-feeding from public indecency statutes. Another five states exempt breastfeeding mothers from jury duty. Three states have enacted provisions that either implement or encourage the development of a breast-feeding awareness education campaign. For more detailed information, see CRS RL31633, A Summary of State Breast Feeding Laws.

## Observations on the Promotion of Breast-Feeding

There is substantial evidence that breast-feeding of infants for 6 months, and perhaps as much as a year, has significant health benefits to the child. There also seems to be evidence that mothers benefit as well. However, less clear is the impact of programs to promote breast-feeding on the rates of breast-feeding initiation and duration. While the rates of initiation are up compared to the rates in the 1970s, these numbers are not maintained at 6 and 12 months of age, at the level current health guidelines would suggest for attaining maximum benefit for the child.

In Healthy People 2010, the federal government has set a goal of increasing rates of breast-feeding. Providing mothers and their children with the necessary support for successful breast-feeding might contribute to the achievement of this goal. Various options that have been suggested, include greater support in the workplace, extended paid maternity leave, job-sharing or other part-time employment, better training for health care professionals in working with pregnant and lactating women, and providing better coordination among government policies that promote women working and breast-feeding. However, given the difficulty experienced by many women of simultaneously balancing the demands of employment and breast-feeding, it is not possible to estimate the potential of these options in increasing the rate of breast-feeding toward meeting the national goals

## References


[1] Jon Weimer, U.S. Dept. of Agriculture, Economic Research Service, *The Economic Benefits of Breast Feeding: A Review and Analysis*. Food Assistance and Nutrition Research report no. 13, Mar. 2001, 14 pp. (Hereafter cited as Weimer, *The Economic Benefits of Breast Feeding*.)

[2] A.S. Ryan, *The Resurgence of Breastfeeding in the United States*, Pediatrics, vol. 99, no. 4, Apr. 1997, p. 12.

[3] U.S. Department of Health and Human Services, Office of the Assistant Secretary for Health, Healthy People 2010, vol. I and II. (Washington, GPO), Jan. 2000.

[4] U. S. Department of Health and Human Services, Health People 2010, Washington, D.C., 2000.

[5] "Vitamins Urged for Breast-fed Babies." Pediatricians recommend vitamin D to prevent rickets. *The Washington Post*, Apr. 7, 2003, p. A5.

[6] National Academy of Sciences, Institute of Medicine, Food and Nutrition Board, *Nutrition During Lactation,* Committee on Nutritional Status During Pregnancy and Lactation, Subcommittee on Nutrition During Lactation, National Academy Press, 1991. (Hereafter cited as National Academy of Sciences, *Nutrition During Lactation*).

[7] L.A. Hanson, Human Milk and Host Defense. Immediate and Long-term Effects, Acta Paediatric Supplement, vol. 88, no. 430, Aug. 1999 pp. 42-46.

[8] National Academy of Sciences, *Nutrition During Lactation.*

[9] J.M. Heinig and K.G. Dewey, "Health Effects of Breast Feeding fo Mothers: A Critical Review," *Nutrition Research Review*, 1997, vol 10, 1997, pp. 35-56.

[10] Abbott Laboratories, Ross Products Division, Ensuring Optimal Infan Nutrition: A Shared Responsibility, Apr. 2003, 12 pp.

[11] Jon Weimer, *The Economic Benefits of Breast-feeding.*

[12] T.M. Ball and A. L. Wright, "Health Care Costs of Formula-feeding in the First Year of Life," *Pediatrics*, vol. 103, no. 4, Apr. 1999, pp. 870-876.
[13] D. Montgomery and P. Splett, "Economic Benefit of Breast-Feeding Infants Enrolled in WIC," *Journal of American Dietetic Association*, vol. 97, no. 4, Apr. 1997, pp. 379-385.
[14] C.M. Visness and K.I. Kennedy, "Maternal Employment and Breastfeeding: Findings Form the 1988 National Maternal and Infant Health Survey," *American Journal of Public Health*, vol. 87, no. 6, June 1997, pp. 945-950.
[15] B. Roe, et al., "Is There Competition Between Breast-feeding and Maternal Employment?," *Demography*, vol. 36, no. 2 May 1999, pp. 157-171.
[16] S.B. Fein, and B. Roe, "The Effect of Work Status on Initiation and Duration of Breastfeeding," *American Journal of Public Health*, vol. 88, no. 7, July 1998, pp. 1042-1046.
[17] K. Tyler, "Got Milk? Breastfeeding Programs," *Human Resources Management Magazine*, vol. 44. Mar. 1, 1999, p. 68.
[18] A.L. Wright, "The Rise of Breastfeeding in the United States," *Pediatrics Clinical North America.*, vol. 48, no. 1, Feb. 2001, pp. 1-12.
[19] R. Zetterstrom,"Breastfeeding and Infant-mother Interaction," *Acta Paediatric Supplement*, v. 88, no. 430. Aug. 1999, pp. 1-6.
[20] Armstrong, H. *UNICEF: Lessons Learned from the Baby-Friendly Hospital Initiative,* in Women Friendly Health Services — Experiences in Maternal Care: A Report of a WHO/UNICEF/UNFPA Workshop, Mexico City, Jan. 28, 1999.
[21] U.S. Department of Health and Human Services, Office of Women's Health, Breastfeeding: HHS Blueprint for Act on Breastfeeding, 2000, 32 pp

In: Breastfeeding: Laws and Societal Impact ISBN 1-59454-754-8
Editor: Sarah W. Ying, pp. 15-55 

*Chapter 2*

# HHS BLUEPRINT FOR ACTION ON BREASTFEEDING

***Department of Health and Human Services***

## A MESSAGE FROM THE SURGEON GENERAL

Breastfeeding is one of the most important contributors to infant health. Breastfeeding provides a range of benefits for the infant's growth, immunity, and development [1]. In addition, breastfeeding improves maternal health and contributes economic benefits to the family, health care system, and workplace [2].

Despite the many benefits of breastfeeding, the rates of breastfeeding in the United States are low, especially at 6 months postpartum. In 1998, the year for which the most recent statistics are available, only 29% of all mothers breastfed at 6 months postpartum [3]. Moreover, racial and ethnic disparities in breastfeeding rates are wide and reveal alarmingly low breastfeeding rates among African American women (19% at 6 months postpartum) [3]. The nation must address these low breastfeeding rates as a public health challenge and put in place national, culturally appropriate strategies to promote breastfeeding.

During the past 15 years, the Office of the Surgeon General has highlighted the public health importance of breastfeeding through numerous workshops and publications. In 1984, the Office of the Surgeon General held the first workshop on breastfeeding and human lactation, which made the following recommendations:

- "Improve professional education in human lactation and breastfeeding
- "Develop public education and promotional efforts
- "Strengthen the support for breastfeeding in the health care system
- "Develop a broad range of support services in the community
- "Initiate a national breastfeeding promotion effort directed to women in the world of work
- "Expand research on human lactation and breastfeeding" [4-5].

In 1985 and 1991, reports were developed to describe the various breastfeeding promotion activities that resulted in followup to the Surgeon General's workshop, such as legislation, policies, resolutions, guidelines, meetings, publications, media campaigns, service delivery models, support systems, and research [5-6].

In 1990, the United States recognized the importance of breastfeeding by signing the *Innocenti Declaration on the Protection, Promotion, and Support of Breastfeeding* adopted by the World Health Organization and United Nations Children's Fund (UNICEF)[7]. Concurrently, the U.S. Department of Health and Human Services, through its Healthy People 2000 and subsequently Healthy People 2010, established breastfeeding objectives for the early postpartum period, at 6 months postpartum, and at 1 year postpartum. In addition, recognition of the benefits of breastfeeding has led to the adoption of breastfeeding policies by many health and professional organizations in the United States, including the American Academy of Pediatrics [8], the American College of Obstetricians and Gynecologists [9], the American Academy of Family Physicians [10], the American Dietetic Association [1], the American College of NurseMidwives [12], the National Medical Association [13], and the American Public Health Association [14].

To advance these efforts further, I requested the Office on Women's Health, in conjunction with other Federal agencies and health care professional organizations, to assist me in developing this Blueprint for Action on Breastfeeding. Under the auspices of the Environmental Health Policy Committee, the Office on Women's Health created the Subcommittee on Breastfeeding, consisting of government representatives from various Federal agencies and liaison members from nonfederal organizations (Box 1). This Blueprint for Action establishes a comprehensive breastfeeding policy for the nation.

The Blueprint for Action introduces an action plan for breastfeeding based on education, training, awareness, support and research. The plan includes key recommendations that were refined by the members and reviewers of the Subcommittee on Breastfeeding during their deliberations of sciencebased findings. Recognizing that breastfeeding rates are influenced by various factors, these recommendations suggest an approach in which all interested stakeholders come together to forge partnerships to promote breastfeeding. Each of us, whether we play a role at the Federal, State, local, or private level, must turn these recommendations into programs best suited for our own communities. Together we can shape a future in which mothers can feel comfortable and free to breastfeed their children without societal hindrances. While there has been considerable progress toward reaching this goal, there remains a significant challenge to reach African American women with culturally appropriate approaches to promote breastfeeding.

David Satcher, M.D., Ph.D.
Assistant Secretary for Health
and Surgeon General U.S. Department
of Health and Human Services

| **BOX 1:SUBCOMMITTEE ON BREASTFEEDING Members** | |
|---|---|
| Chairperson: Suzanne G. Haynes, Ph.D. Office on Women's Health U.S. Department of Health and Human Services | Kenneth L. Dominguez, M.D., M.P.H. National Center for HIV, STD, and TB Prevention Centers for Disease Control and Prevention |
| Coordinator: Ekaterini Malliou, M.P.H. Office on Women's Health U.S. Department of Health and Human Services | Sara Fein, Ph.D. Center for Food Safety and Applied Nutrition Food and Drug Administration |
| Sharon Adamo, M.S., M.B.A., R.D. Food and Nutrition Services U.S. Department of Agriculture | Scott Grosse, Ph.D. National Center for Environmental Health Centers for Disease Control and Prevention |
| Laina Bush, M.B.A. Office of the Assistant Secretary for Planning and Evaluation U.S. Department of Health and Human Services | Laurence GrummerStrawn, Ph.D. National Center for Chronic Disease Prevention and Health Promotion Centers for Disease Control and Prevention |

Jean CharlesAzure, Ph.D. Indian Health Service U.S. Department of Health and Human Services

Eileen Choffness, Ph.D. Office of Science Coordination and Policy Environmental Protection Agency

Margarett K. Davis, M.D., M.P.H. National Center for Chronic Disease Prevention and Health Promotion Centers for Disease Control and Prevention

Kathryn S. DawsKopp Center for Devices and Radiological Health Food and Drug Administration

Insun Kim, Dr.P.H. National Center for Health Statistics Centers for Disease Control and Prevention

Miriam H. Labbok, M.D., M.P.H. Nutrition and Maternal/Infant Health Division U.S. Agency for International Development

Ernestine W. Murray, R.N, M.A.S. Center for Practice and Technology Assessment Agency for Healthcare Research and Quality

Richard Rheingans, Ph.D. Division of Health Education and Promotion Agency for Toxic Substances and Disease Registry

Susie Humphreys, Ph.D. Center for Food Safety and Applied Nutrition Food and Drug Administration

Wanda K. Jones, Dr.P.H. Office on Women's Health U.S. Department of Health and Human Services

Mireille B. Kanda, M.D., M.P.H. Health and Disabilities Services Administration for Children and Families

Woodie Kessel, M.D. Office of Disease Prevention and Health Promotion U.S. Department of Health and Human Services

Mona Rowe, M.C.P. National Institute of Child Health and Human Development National Institutes of Health

Margaret Scarlett, D.M.D. Office of HIV/AIDS Policy U.S. Department of Health and Human Services

Phillip L. Smith, M.D., M.P.H. Indian Health Service U.S. Department of Health and Human Services

Denise M. Sofka, M.P.H., R.D. Maternal and Child Health Bureau Health Resources and Services Administration

| | |
|---|---|
| Walter Rogan, M.D. National Institute of Environmental Health Sciences National Institutes of Health | Susanne Strickland, M.S., R.D. National Institute of Child Health and Human Development National Institutes of Health |
| Heather S. Rosecrans Center for Drug Evaluation and Research Food and Drug Administration | Naomi G. Swanson, Ph.D. National Institute for Occupational Safety and Health Centers for Disease Control and Prevention |
| Jonelle Rowe, M.D. Office on Women's Health U.S. Department of Health and Human Services | Karen Winer, M.D. National Institute of Child Health and Human Development National Institutes of Health |

| **BOX 1:SUBCOMMITTEE ON BREASTFEEDING Liaison Members Reviewers** | |
|---|---|
| Lois D. W. Arnold, M.P.H., I.B.C.L.C. National Commission on Donor Milk Banking | Linda Lange, Dr.P.H., R.N. University of California, Los Angeles |
| Linda Black, M.D. American Academy of Pediatrics | Ruth Lawrence, M.D. University of Rochester School of Medicine |
| Yvonne Bronner, Sc.D., R.D., L.D. Morgan State University | James H. Lindenberger, I.B.C.L.C. Best Start Social Marketing |
| Karin Cadwell, Ph.D., R.N, I.B.C.L.C. Healthy Children 2000 | Elaine Locke, M.P.A. American College of Obstetricians and Gynecologists |
| Jan Chapin, R.N., M.P.H. American College of Obstetricians and Gynecologists | Teresa Marchese, C.N.M., Ph.D., F.A.C.N.M. American College of NurseMidwives |
| Sheila Clark, M.S.W. National Black Women's Health Project | Karen Sherwood, M.S., M.B.A. American Association of Health Plans |
| Joyce Dougherty, Ph.D., M.S. Washington State Department of Health | |

| | |
|---|---|
| Julianna S. Gonen, Ph.D. Washington Business Group on Health | Cindy TurnerMaffei, M.A., I.B.C.L.C. Baby Friendly USA |
| Millicent Gorham, M.B.A. National Black Nurses Association | Patricia Underwood, Ph.D., R.N. American Nurses Association |
| Barbara Heiser, R.N., B.S.N., I.B.C.L.C. National Alliance for Breastfeeding Advocacy | Joy Johnson Wilson, M.R.P. National Conference of State Legislatures |
| Bonnie Connors Jellen, M.A. American Hospital Association | Julie Wood, M.D. Academy of Family Physicians |
| Linda J. Smith, B.S.E., F.A.C.C.E., I.B.C.L.C. Coalition for Improving Maternity Services | Michael Young, M.D. National Medical Association |

## BREASTFEEDING AS A PUBLIC HEALTH CHALLENGE

Breastfeeding is the ideal method of feeding and nurturing infants:

- Breast milk is the most complete form of nutrition for infants.
- Breastfeeding protects an infant from a wide array of infectious and noninfectious diseases.
- Breastfeeding improves maternal health by reducing postpartum bleeding and may lower the risk of premenopausal breast cancer and ovarian cancer.

Despite the wellrecognized benefits of breastfeeding, the Healthy People 2000 goals for breastfeeding were not met [23]. These goals were to increase to 75% the proportion of mothers who breastfeed their babies in the early postpartum period, and to increase to 50% the proportion of mothers who breastfeed their babies through 5 to 6 months of age [3]. In 1998, 64% of all mothers breastfed in the early postpartum period and only 29% breastfed at 6 months postpartum [3].

One of the two major goals of Healthy People 2010 is to eliminate health disparities among different segments of the population [3]. Racial and ethnic disparities in breastfeeding are wide despite substantial increases in breastfeeding rates in the last decade [15]. In 1998, 45% of African American mothers breastfed their infants in the early postpartum period; 66% of Hispanic mothers and 68% of white mothers did so. Furthermore, in 1998, 54% of lowincome Asian and Pacific Islander children and 59% of lowincome American Indian and Alaska native children were ever breastfed [16].

**Box 2: Definitions**

**Breastfeeding:** The Institute of Medicine report *Nutrition During Lactation* applies the term "exclusive breastfeeding" when infants are fed only by this method; "partial breastfeeding" when breastfeeding is supplemented with limited amounts of formula, juice, water, or solid foods; and "minimal breastfeeding" when the infant receives nearly all sustenance from formula and other foods [1]. In this HHS document, "breastfeeding" and "human milk" are interchangeable terms.

**Human Lactation:** The process of milk production in which human milk is secreted by the mammary glands, which are located within the fatty tissue of the breasts.

**Healthy People 2000:** A national cooperative effort by government agencies and voluntary and professional organizations to improve the health of all Americans by establishing health objectives and measuring progress toward those objectives. Its purpose is to promote health and prevent disease through changes in lifestyle and other factors. Healthy People 2000 set three broad goals to: 1. Increase the span of healthy lives for Americans, 2. Reduce health disparities among Americans, and 3. Achieve access to preventive services for all Americans [2].

**Healthy People 2010:** Contains broad reaching national health goals for the new decade, focusing on two major themes: 1. Increase quality and years of healthy life, and 2. Eliminate health disparities [3].

*This document presents the consensus of the members and reviewers on the HHS Subcommittee on Breastfeeding; it does not necessarily reflect the policy of the nonfederal representative organizations.*

No group of women reached the goal of breastfeeding for 5 to 6 months postpartum (50%), and again, disparities exist across racial and ethnic groups (19% of African American mothers, 28% of Hispanic mothers, and 31% of white mothers breastfed). (See Box 3).

In Healthy People 2010, an additional objective was added for 25% of mothers to breastfeed their babies through the end of 1 year [3]. Only 9% of African American mothers met this objective in 1998, whereas 17% of Hispanic and 19% white mothers met the goal.

**Box 3: Racial and Ethnic Disparities in Breastfeeding Rates and Healthy People 2010 Breastfeeding Objectives for the Nation [3]**

| Objective: Increase the proportion of mothers who breastfeed their babies | 1998 Baseline Percent (%) | 2010 Target |
|---|---|---|
| In early postpartum period | | |
| All women | 64 | 75 |
| Black or African American | 45 | 75 |
| Hispanic or Latino | 66 | 75 |
| White | 68 | 75 |
| At 6 months | | |
| All women | 29 | 50 |
| Black or African American | 19 | 50 |
| Hispanic or Latino | 28 | 50 |
| White | 31 | 50 |
| At 1 year | | |
| All women | 16 | 25 |
| Black or African American | 9 | 25 |
| Hispanic or Latino | 19 | 25 |
| White | 17 | 25 |

A number of reasons might explain why so few African American mothers breastfeed. Breastfeeding is not viewed positively among African American women [17]. Furthermore, it has been difficult for African American women to receive information and education about breastfeeding to have breastfeeding initiated in the hospital, to continue breastfeeding in the early days in the home setting, and to continue breastfeeding for an extended period [17].

Increasing the rates of breastfeeding is a compelling public health goal particularly among the racial and ethnic groups who are less likely to initiate and sustain breastfeeding throughout the infant's first year [3].

Significant steps must be taken to increase breastfeeding rates in the United States and to close the wide racial and ethnic gaps in breastfeeding. This goal can only be achieved by supporting breastfeeding in the family, community, workplace, health care sector, and society. This Blueprint for Action introduces a comprehensive framework to increase breastfeeding rates in the United States and to promote cptimal breast-feeding practices.

## BENEFITS OF BREASTFEEDING

Extensive research on the biology of human milk and on the health outcomes associated with breastfeeding has established that breastfeeding is more beneficial than formula feeding. Breastfed infants experience fewer cases of infectious and noninfectious diseases as well as less severe cases of diarrhea, respiratory infections, and ear infections [18-32]. Mothers who breastfeed experience less postpartum bleeding, earlier return to pre-pregnancy weight, and a reduced risk of ovarian cancer and premenopausal breast cancer [33-43]. Furthermore, breastfeeding is costbeneficial to families [26]. Based on this evidence, the American Academy of Pediatrics has stated that "The breastfed infant is the reference or normative model against which all alternative feeding methods must be measured with regard to growth, health, development, and all other short- and long-term outcomes" [8]. Thus, human milk is uniquely suited for human infants.

### Resistance to Infectious Diseases

Human milk contains an abundance of factors that are active against infection. Since the infant's immune system is not fully mature until about 2 years of age, the transfer of these factors from human milk provides a distinct advantage that infants fed formula do not experience. Specifically, human milk contains immunologic agents and other compounds, such as secretory antibodies, leukocytes, and carbohydrates, that act against viruses, bacteria, and parasites [44-45]. Overall, research shows that breastfeeding may decrease the incidence of several acute bacterial and viral infections in infants (Box 4).

**Box 4: Infections that Are Lower in Incidence or Severity in Breastfed Infants than in Formula-fed Infants**

- Diarrhea (18, 21, 29-30, 46)
- Respiratory tract infection (18, 21, 46-49)
- Otitis media (19, 29, 50-51)
- Pneumonia (52-53)
- Urinary infection (54-55)
- Necrotizing enterocolitis [56-57]
- Invasive bacterial infection [44, 59-61]

## Enhanced Immune System

Breastfed infants, compared with formula-fed infants, produce enhanced immune responses to polio, tetanus, diphtheria, and Haemophilus influenzae immunizations, and to respiratory syncytial virus infection, a common infant respiratory infection [44, 62-63]. Human milk contains anti-inflammatory factors and other factors that regulate the response of the immune system against infection [44]. There is also evidence that breastfeeding results in earlier development of the infant immune system [64].

Protection against infection is strongest during the first several months of life for infants who are breastfed exclusively [19, 21, 29, 46-48, 59]. Several studies suggest that the benefits continue even after breastfeeding ceases [19, 21, 61], and a few studies have found that breastfeeding into the second 6 months of life protects against infection [29-30, 52]. Longer durations of breastfeeding may provide an even stronger protective effect [19, 21, 51, 61, 65]. Finally, children who were breastfed exclusively have fewer illnesses than those who were never breastfed [19, 46, 48].

## Nutritional and Growth Benefits

Human milk contains a balance of nutrients that more closely match human infant requirements for growth and development than does the milk of any other species [66]. For example, compared to cow's milk, human milk is low in total protein and low in casein, making it more readily digestible and less stressful on immature infant kidneys. The lipids and enzymes human milk promote efficient digestion and utilization of nutrients [66-67].

Scientific evidence suggests that the normal pattern for breastfed infants is to gain less weight and to be leaner at 1 year of age than formula-fed infants, while maintaining normal activity level and development [68]. This early growth pattern may influence later growth patterns, resulting in less overweight and obesity among children who were breastfed [68-76]. Despite the finding that many African American infants are premature or small at birth, premature babies fare better when breastfed compared to premature babies who are fed formula [69, 77].

## Reduced Risk for Chronic Diseases

Many studies in infant feeding have found lower rates of several chronic childhood diseases among children who were breastfed. Recent findings suggest that breastfeeding may reduce the risk of type 1 and 2 diabetes [78-82], celiac disease [83-85, 87], inflammatory bowel disease [88-90=, childhood cancer [28, 91-92], and allergic disease/asthma [32, 96-100. Mixed results from some studies suggest that further research is needed to establish some of these benefits [86, 93-95.

## Developmental Benefits

Considerable interest has been raised about the potential effect of breastfeeding on cognitive development [101-107]. Longchain polyunsaturated fatty acids, available in breast milk, are important for brain growth and development [103-107]. Observations in some studies on neurological and cognitive outcomes in breastfed children have led to a hypothesis that the early visual acuity and cognitive function of these children is greater than in nonbreastfed children [101, 104-105]. However, this hypothesis has not been conclusively proven [102,106].

## Improved Maternal Health

Breastfeeding has several positive hormonal, physical, and psychosocial effects on the mother. Breastfeeding increases levels of oxytocin, a hormone that stimulates uterine contractions, helping to expel the placenta, to minimize postpartum maternal blood loss, and to induce a more rapid uterine involution [1, 108]. Breastfeeding, particularly exclusive breastfeeding, delays the resumption of normal ovarian cycles and the return of fertility in most women [109]. Mothers who breastfeed their infants may also experience psychological benefits, such as increased selfconfidence and facilitated bonding with their infants [110-112]. Studies have shown that breastfeeding for longer time periods (up to 2 years) and among younger mothers (early 20s) may reduce the risk of premenopausal and possibly postmenopausal breast cancer [35-40, 113]. In addition, the risk of ovarian cancer may be lower among women who have breastfed their children [41-43].

### Socioeconomic Benefits

Breastfeeding provides economic and social benefits to the family, the health care system, the employer, and the nation [114]. Families can save several hundred dollars over the cost of feeding breast milk sub stitutes, even after accounting for the costs of breast pump equipment and additional food required by the nursing mother [115]. Breastfed infants typically require fewer sick care visits, prescriptions, and hospitalizations, especially if breastfed exclusively or almost exclusively [26]. Consequently, total medical care expenditures were about 20% lower for fully breastfed infants than for neverbreastfed infants [116]. Because of the high occurrence of poverty among African Americans, these families would benefit substantially from breastfeeding their infants [117].

Employers also benefit when their employees breastfeed. Breastfe infants are sick less often; therefore, maternal absenteeism from work i significantly lower in companies with established lactation programs [118 In addition, employer medical costs are lower and employee productivity i higher.

## Cautions about Breastfeeding

Human milk provides the most complete form of nutrition for infant including premature and sick newborns, with rare exceptions [8]. Wh direct breastfeeding is not possible, expressed human milk, fortified wh necessary for the premature infant, should be provided [8]. Professio health care advice against breastfeeding or recommendations abc premature weaning should be based on a careful consideration of the gene benefits of breastfeeding, the risks of not receiving human milk, and the most uptodate information about the following situations.

Under certain conditions, women should not breastfeed:

- HIVinfected women in the United States should not breastfeed or provide their breast milk for the nutrition of their own or other infants because of the risk of HIV transmission to the child [119-121]. In countries with populations at increased risk for other infectious diseases and nutritional deficiencies resulting in infant death, the mortality risks associated with not breastfeeding may outweigh the possible risk of transmission of HIV infection [8].
- Women with human Tcell leukemia virus type 1 (HTLV1) should not breastfeed because of the risk of transmission to the child [122].

Under certain conditions, a casebycase assessment should be made of whether or not breastfeeding is advisable or should be temporarily suspended. A physician should evaluate cases involving:

- **Environmental Exposures:** During the last 30 years, environmental chemicals, such as polychlorinated biphenyls (PCBs), DDT, dioxin, methyl mercury, and lead have appeared in breast milk without ocupational or even known exposure on the part of the woman (Appendix 1) [123]. Although most women have detectable levels of these agents, there are no established "normal" or "abnormal" values for clinical interpretation; therefore, breast milk is not routinely tested for these environmental pollutants. Thus far, effects on the nursing child have been seen primarily in poisonings where the mother herself was clinically ill [124].

Advisories are issued by the states, U.S. territories, Native American ibes, and the Environmental Protection Agency to inform residents of otential health risks from consuming contaminated noncommercially aught fish and wildlife. These advisories identify specific fish and wildlife ecies from specific water bodies [125]. These fish advisories should be llowed.

- **Hepatitis C:** Transmission of hepatitis C through breast milk has not been established. The risk of infection among infants of infected mothers is the same whether breast or bottle fed. However, bleeding or cracked nipples on the breast of a woman positive for hepatitis C may put a breastfeeding infant at risk for transmission of hepatitis C [126].

- **Illicit Drugs:** Amphetamines, cocaine, heroin, marijuana, and phencyclidine should not be ingested by the nursing mother. Not only are they hazardous to the nursing infant, but also they are detrimental to the physical and emotional health of the mother. This list is not complete; no drug of abuse should be ingested by nursing mothers even in the absence of adverse reports in the literature [127-128].
- **Implants and Breast Surgery:** It is not known whether breastfeeding by women who have breast implants has an effect on the nursing infant [129]. Many women with implants lactate successfully. Women who have had reduction mammoplasty may not be able to lactate if the glandular tissue has been removed or the connection between it and the nipple is interrupted.
- **Metabolic Disorders:** An infant born with galactosemia cannot metabolize lactose, a sugar found in all mammalian milk. Such infants must be fed plantderived formula [130]. Infants with phenylketonuria can be successfully breastfed, but doing so requires special clinical management [131].
- **Pharmaceutical Drugs:** For most prescribed and overthecounter medications taken by women, the risk to the nursing infant is unknown. A few medications make it necessary to discontinue breastfeeding.

For example, cyclophosphamide, cyclosporin, doxorubicin, ergotamine methotrexate, and radioactive isotopes are prohibited during lactation [8 127]. Pharmaceutical drugs that effect the central nervous system, such a antianxiety, antidepressant, and antipsychotic agents, are of special concer when taken by nursing mothers [127]. Some pharmaceutical agents such a bromocriptine and possibly estrogens in contraceptive doses mak breastfeeding more difficult because they decrease breast milk productio and consequently shorten breastfeeding duration [127]. A woman taking an of those drugs should not breastfeed without first consulting her health ca provider.

- **Tobacco and Alcohol Consumption:** Alcohol appears in brea milk [132-133]. For this reason, and for the general health of t mother, if alcohol is used, intake should be limited. The Americ Academy of Pediatrics Committee on Drugs lists alcohol "usually compatible with breastfeeding" [127]. Nursing mothers should not smoke. Nicotine is present in the breast milk of smokers and may adversely affect milk volume [134]. However, for women who cannot or will not stop smoking, breastfeeding is still advisable, since the benefits of breast milk outweigh the risks from nicotine exposure.

## Facilitation and Support for Breastfeeding

A woman's ability to optimally breastfeed her infant depends on the support she receives from those around her. Several factors and contexts facilitate the initiation and continuation of breastfeeding; others may pose barriers. The overriding principle is to make breastfeeding as easy as possible for the mother rather than to discourage her from breastfeeding, either intentionally or unintentionally.

### Health Care System

The health care system has an important role to play in the promotion and support of breastfeeding [135-140]. Breastfeeding support is particularly critical in the first few weeks postpartum, as lactation is being established [141]. Therefore, all breastfeeding mothers must have access to lactation management support provided by trained physicians, nurses, lactation specialists, peer counselors, and other trained health care providers, especially during the first days and weeks postpartum [142].

All health care providers who interact with women or infants should be knowledgeable about the basics of lactation and the role their specialty plays in breastfeeding [135-140]. Providers of maternal and child health care have a special role in the promotion of breastfeeding during the prenatal and postnatal periods. They must be knowledgeable and skillful in counseling women about breastfeeding and lactation, and in providing medical care to breastfeeding mothers and their babies. To this end, culturally appropriate training for breastfeeding should be integrated into the curricula of health profession schools. Special attention should be given to barriers to breastfeeding for all women, especially African American and other minority women [143]. Breastfeeding training should also be provided under the continuing education requirements for practitioners.

Early experience with breastfeeding is critical, and nonsupportive hospital experiences and lack of support from health care providers have been identified as barriers to breastfeeding, especially among African American women [17]. Therefore, maternity care and newborn facilities should follow practices conducive to proper lactation [144-145] even when inhospital maternity care is of short duration. For example, hospitals and other maternity centers are encouraged to adopt the "Ten Steps to Successful Breastfeeding" as outlined by the United Nations Children's Fund, the World Health Organization, the Breastfeeding Hospital Initiative Feasibility Study Expert Work Group, and Baby Friendly USA [146-149] (Box 5). Furthermore, the 1984 Surgeon General's Workshop on Breastfeeding and Human Lactation recommended several hospital practices, presented in Box 6, which influence breastfeeding initiation and are important during hospital stays [4].

**Box 5: Practices for Successful Breastfeeding Services at Hospital and Maternity Centers [146-149]**

- A written breastfeeding policy that is communicated to all healthcare staff
- Staff training in the skills needed to implement the policy
- Education of pregnant women about the benefits and management of breastfeeding
- Early initiation of breastfeeding
- Education of mothers on how to breastfeed and maintain lactation
- Limited use of any food or drink other than human breast milk
- Roomingin
- Breastfeeding on demand
- Limited use of pacifiers and artificial nipples
- Fostering of breastfeeding support groups and services

**Box 6: Hospital Practices Which Influence Breastfeeding Initiation [4]**

| ←Strongly Encouraging → | ←Encouraging → | ←Discouraging → | ←Strongly Discouraging→ |
|---|---|---|---|
| **Physical Contact** | | | |
| • baby put to breast immediately in delivery room<br>• baby not taken from mother after delivery<br>• woman helped by staff to suckle baby in recovery room<br>• rooming in; staff help with baby care in room, not only in nursery | • staff sensitivity to cultural norms and expectations of woman | • scheduled feedings regardless of mother's breastfeeding wishes | • mother infant separation at birth<br>• mother infant housed on separate floors in post partum period<br>• mother separated from baby due to bilirubin problem<br>• no rooming in policy |
| **Verbal Communication** | | | |
| • staff initiates discussion re: woman's intention to breastfeed pre and intrapartum<br>• staff encourages and reinforces breast feeding immediately on labor and delivery<br>• staff discusses use of breast pump and realities of separation from baby, re: breastfeeding<br>• pictures of woman breastfeeding | • appropriate language skills of staff, teaching how to handle breast engorgement and nipple problem<br>• | • staff instructs woman "to get good night's rest and miss the feed"<br>• | • woman told to "take it easy," "get your rest" . . . impression that breastfeeding is effortful/ tiring<br>• woman told she doesn't "do it right," staff interrupts her efforts, corrects her re: positions, etc. |

**Box 6: Hospital Practices Which Influence Breastfeeding Initiation [4] (Continued)**

| ←Strongly Encouraging → | ←Encouraging → | ←Discouraging → | ←Strongly Discouraging→ |
|---|---|---|---|
| • literature on breastfeeding in understandable terms | • staff's own skills and comfort re: art of breastfeeding and time to teach woman on one to one basis | • strict times allotted for breast feeding regardless of mother/ baby's feeding "cycle" | |
| **Non Verbal Communication** | | | |
| • staff (doctors as well as nurses) give reinforcement for breastfeeding (respect, smiles, affirmation)<br>• nurse (or any attendant) making mother comfortable and helping to arrange baby at breast for nursing<br>• woman sees others breastfeeding in hospital | • closed circuit TV shown in hospital on breastfeeding | • pictures of woman bottle feeding<br>• staff interrupts her breastfeeding session for lab tests, etc.<br>• woman doesn't see others breastfeeding | • woman given infant formula kit and infant food literature<br>• woman sees official looking nurses authoritatively caring for babies by bottle feeding (leads to woman's insecurities re: own capability of care) |

**Box 6: Hospital Practices Which Influence Breastfeeding Initiation [4] (Continued)**

| ←Strongly Encouraging → | ←Encouraging → | ←Discouraging → | ←Strongly Discouraging→ |
|---|---|---|---|
| **Experiential** | | | |
| • if breastfeeding not immediately successful, staff continues to be supportive<br>• previous success with breastfeeding experience in hospital | | | • previous failure with breastfeeding experience in hospital |

## The Workplace

A large proportion (70%) of employed mothers who have children under 3 years of age work full time [150]. About onethird of these mothers return to work within 3 months and about twothirds within 6 months after the baby is born [151-152]. However, African American women are more likely than other women to return to work earlier (8 weeks) and to be engaged in jobs that do not allow the mother to be successful at breastfeeding [153]. The workplace environment should enable mothers to continue breastfeeding as long as the mother and baby desire. Worksite programs that support breastfeeding will facilitate the continuation of breastfeeding after mothers return to their jobs [154-155]. Such programs include:

- "Prenatal lactation education specifically tailored for "working women
- "Corporate policies providing information for all "employees on the benefits of breastfeeding and "services available to support breastfeeding women
- "Education for personnel about why their breastfeed ing coworkers need support
- "Adequate breaks, flexible work hours, job sharing "and parttime work
- "Private "Mother's Rooms" for expressing milk in a "secure and relaxing environment
- "Access to hospitalgrade, autocycling breast pumps at the workplace
- "Small refrigerators for safe storage of breast milk
- "Subsidization or purchase of individually owned "portable breast pumps for employees
- "Access to a lactation professional onsite or by phone to give breastfeeding education, counseling and support during pregnancy after delivery and when the mother returns to work
- "Coordination with onsite or nearsite child care "programs so infants can be breastfed during the day
- "Support groups for working mothers with children" "[156].

## Childcare Facilities

With a large number of infants enrolled in childcare, it is also important that childcare facilities be supportive of breastfeeding [157]. Childcare centers should make accommodations for mothers who wish to breastfeed their children or have their children fed expressed milk at the facility.

## Public Education and Support

All breastfeeding women and their partners need reliable and culturally appropriate sources of information and social support for breastfeeding [158-159]. Depending on a woman's needs, various levels of skill and training may be called for, from lactation consultants or specialists to peer counselors to other mothers who have breastfed [160]. Women may access information through books, web pages, information phone lines, hotlines, home visits, prenatal/postpartum classes, or mother-to-mother support groups.

Social support, particularly peer support, is critical for special populations with lower breastfeeding rates (e.g., African Americans, teen mothers) [161-162]. More broadly, the views and perceptions of those interacting with a woman can affect her view on breastfeeding, particularly those of the infant's father [141]. Health education in schools should include information on the importance of breastfeeding for children's and women's health. Educational campaigns should be directed toward fathers, especially African American fathers, and other family members (e.g., grandmothers) who greatly influence the woman's decision to breastfeed [141, 163-167].

A public health social marketing effort is needed to increase breastfeeding rates. In addition to culturally appropriate interventions, the social marketing effort would include a media campaign which presents images of breastfeeding as the normal way to feed infants in most places women and their infants go [168-169].

## Marketing of Breast Milk Substitutes

The marketing of infant formula negatively affects breastfeeding [142, 170-172]. The International Code of Marketing of Breast Milk Substitutes and a subsequent WHO resolution delineates guidelines for formula marketing to ensure that it does not interfere with the establishment of lactation [173]. The International Code stipulates the responsibilities of manufacturing industries regarding their role in promoting breastfeeding and appropriate infant feeding practices.

## Major HHS Breastfeeding Activities in the 1990s

Since the 1991 followup to the Surgeon General's Workshop on Breastfeeding and Human Lactation, much has happened to advance the promotion, protection, and support of breastfeeding for families in the United States. In the 1990s, HHS supported the establishment of the United States Breastfeeding Committee (USBC). As a collaborative publicprivate partnership of about 30 major organizations, the USBC was created to satisfy one of the goals identified in the *Innocenti Declaration:* "Establishing of a multisectoral national breastfeeding committee composed of representatives from relevant government departments, nongovernmental organizations, and health professional associations" [7]. In November 1998, HHS cosponsored the National Breastfeeding Policy Conference in Washington, D.C., which generated recommendations for setting a national policy agenda to promote, protect, and support breastfeeding well into the 21st century. Many of the themes that emerged from the 1984 Surgeon General's Workshop on Breastfeeding and Human Lactation continued as a thread throughout this conference.

HHS, through the Health Resources and Services Administration' Maternal and Child Health Bureau, requested that the USBC provide strategic plan to implement this policy agenda. The breastfeeding strategi plan (Appendix 2) sets forth goals and objectives to improve breastfeedin initiation and duration, to reduce and remove barriers to breastfeeding, t provide equitable access to lactation care and services, and to promot breastfeeding as the cultural norm for infant and child feeding [174]. Th USBC strategic plan for breastfeeding was closely reviewed and considere during the development of the Blueprint for Action.

HHS agencies support breastfeeding through a variety of programs. Th Health Resources and Services Administration provides substantial suppc for breastfeeding provider training and research. The Centers for Disea Control and Prevention plays a major role in supporting breastfeedi nationally through applied research, program evaluation, and surveillan The National Institutes of Health provides substantial support breastfeeding research, totaling $13 million in FY 1998. The Food and Dr

Adminstration regulates manufacturers of breast pumps and ensures their safety and effectiveness. This includes a review of design performance, labeling instructions, and applications.

## BLUEPRINT FOR ACTION ON BREASTFEEDING

Infants should be exclusively breastfed during the first 4 to 6 months of life [175], preferably for a full 6 months [89]. Ideally, breastfeeding should continue through the first year of life [89, 175]. This Blueprint for Action reaffirms the scientific evidence that breastfeeding is the best method for feeding most newborns, and that breastfeeding is beneficial to the infant's and the mother's health. Achieving an increase in the proportion of mothers who breastfeed their babies will require the collaboration of Federal agencies, State and local governments, communities, health professional organizations, advocacy groups, multidisciplinary scientists, industry, health insurers, and the American people. This Blueprint for Action invites all interested stakeholders to forge partnerships for the promotion of breastfeeding. It is also designed to attract broadbased family, community, professional, corporate, and philanthropic participation in order to better focus the public's attention and to motivate actions at the individual and community levels.

Moreover, this Blueprint for Action is directed toward all women and uts across all racial and ethnic populations, socioeconomic classes, ducational groups, and employment arrangements. It concentrates energy in ey breastfeeding promotion domains and denotes responsibility for a efinitive course of action by the various stakeholders to achieve a greater roportion of breastfeeding mothers in American society.

To achieve the Healthy People 2010 Breastfeeding Objectives for the ation (Box 3), the Blueprint for Action recommends that the following eps be taken by the health care system, the workplace, the family, and the ommunity, and identifies several areas of research.

### ealth Care System

- Train health care professionals who provide maternal and child care on the basics of lactation, breastfeeding counseling, and lactation management during coursework, clinical and inservice training, and continuing education.

- Ensure that breastfeeding mothers have access to comprehensive, uptodate, and culturally tailored lactation services provided by trained physicians, nurses, lactation consultants, and nutritionists/ dietitians.
- Establish hospital and maternity center practices that promote breastfeeding, such as the "Ten Steps to Successful Breastfeeding" (Box 5).
- Develop breastfeeding education for women, their partners, and other significant family members during the prenatal and postnatal visits.

## Workplace

- Facilitate breastfeeding or breast milk expression in the workplace by providing private rooms, commerical grade breast pumps, milk storage arrangements, adequate breaks during the day, flexible work schedules, and onsite childcare facilities.
- Establish family and community programs that enable breastfeeding continuation when women return to work in all possible settings.
- Encourage childcare facilities to provide quality breastfeeding support.

## Family and Community

- Develop social support and information resources for breastfeedin women such as hotlines, peer counseling, and mothertomoth support groups.
- Launch and evaluate a public health marketing campaign portrayin breastfeeding as normal, desirable, and achievable.
- Encourage the media to portray breastfeeding as normal, desirab and achievable for women of all cultures and socioeconomic level
- Encourage fathers and other family members to be active involved throughout the breastfeeding experience.

## Research

- Conduct research that identifies the social, cultural, economic, and psychological factors that influence infant feeding behaviors, especially among African American and other minority and ethnic groups.
- Improve the understanding of the health benefits of breastfeeding, especially in reducing the risk for chronic childhood diseases among disadvantaged infants and children.
- Monitor trends on the incidence and duration of exclusive, partial, and minimal breastfeeding, including minority and ethnic groups.
- Compare the costeffectiveness of different programs that promote, protect, and support breastfeeding to ensure optimal use of resources.
- Conduct research to better understand the role of fathers in promoting breastfeeding.
- Evaluate the influence of brief postpartum hospital stays on the initiation and duration of breastfeeding.
- Determine the safety of overthecounter and prescription products taken by lactating women on infant health
- Conduct a large, welldesigned casecontrol study on the effects of breast implants on childhood disorders.

# CONCLUSION

Americans in communities nationwide can make a significant difference n promoting and supporting breastfeeding. The recommendations presented this Blueprint for Action provide an action plan and call for action now. rograms and activities that are implemented and evaluated today will enerate additional recommendations for effective breastfeeding promotion itiatives in the future. A collaborative approach is needed to make progress meeting the Healthy People 2010 breastfeeding goals. The Blueprint for ction is an important step in responding to this major public health allenge of promoting breastfeeding. However, the Healthy People 2010 als will be realized only when society is supportive of breastfeeding, and ly when mothers, especially African American mothers, have been ached with culturally appropriate information and support to breastfeed ir infants.

For further information on breastfeeding and breastfeeding resources, please visit the HHS/OWH website at www.4woman.gov or call 18009949662 or TDD 18882205446.

## ACKNOWLEDGMENTS

The Office on Women's Health would like to acknowledge the following agencies and offices for their contributions: Administration for Children and Families Agency for Healthcare Research and Quality Agency for Toxic Substances and Disease Registry Centers for Disease Control and Prevention Enviromental Protection Agency Food and Drug Administration Health Resources and Services Administration Indian Health Service National Institutes of Health Office of Disease Prevention and Health Promotion Office of HIV/AIDS Policy Office of the Assistant Secretary for Planning and Evaluation U.S. Department of Agriculture U.S. Agency for International Development U.S. Department of Health and Human Services. HHS Blueprint for Action on Breastfeeding, Washington, D.C. U.S. Department of Health and Human Services, Office on Women's Health, 2000. We would also like to acknowledge and thank the Liaison Members of the Subcommittee on Breastfeeding for their important contributions to this Blueprint.

# Appendix 1. Environmental Pollutants That May Be Found in Human Milk [123]

| Chemical Agent | Potential Health Effect |
|---|---|
| DDT, DDE | Estrogenic, antiandrogenic activity |
| PCB/PCDF | Ectodermal defects, developmental delay |
| TCDD (Dioxin) | Chloracne |
| Chlordane | Neurotoxicity |
| Heptachlor | Neurotoxicity |
| Hexachlorobenzene | Hypotonia, seizures, rash |
| Volatile organic compounds: | |
| Tetrachloroethylene | Hepatotoxicity |
| Trichloroethylene | Hepatotoxicity |
| Halothane | Hepatotoxicity |
| Carbon disulfide | Neurotoxicity |
| Nicotine | Neurotoxicity |
| Metal: | |
| Lead | Renal, central nervous system injury |
| Methyl mercury | Central nervous system toxicity |

# Appendix 2. Breastfeeding In The United States: Strategic Plan [174 ]

**Goal 1** Assure access to comprehensive, current and culturally appropriate lactation care and services for all women, children, and families.

- Objective 1.1 Identify and disseminate evidence-based best practices and polices throughout the health care system.
- Objective 1.2 Educate all health care providers and payers regarding appropriate breastfeeding and lactation support.
- Objective 1.3 Ensure that all women have access to appropriate breastfeeding support within the family and/or community.
- Objective 1.4 Ensure the routine collection and coordination of breastfeeding data by Federal, State, and local government and other organizations, and foster additional research of breastfeeding.

**Goal 2** Ensure that breastfeeding is recognized as the normal and preferred method of feeding infants and young children.

- Objective 2.1 Develop a positive and desirable image of breastfeeding for the American public.
- Objective 2.2 Reduce the barriers to breastfeeding posed by the marketing of breast milk substitutes.

**Goal 3** Ensure that all Federal, State, and local laws relating to child welfare and family law recognize and support the importance and practice of breastfeeding.

- Objective 3.1 Ensure that all lawmakers and government officials at Federal, State, and local levels are aware of the importance of protecting, promoting, and supporting breastfeeding.

**Goal 4** Increase protection, promotion, and support for breastfeeding mothers in the work force.

- Objective 4.1 The rights of women in the workplace will be recognized in public and private sectors.
- Objective 4.2 Ensure that all mothers are able to seamlessly integrate breastfeeding and employment.

## REFERENCES

[1] Institute of Medicine. *Nutrition During Lactation.* Washington, DC National Academy Press, 1991, pp. 2425, 161171, 197200.

[2] U.S. Department of Health and Human Services. *Healthy Peop 2000: National Health Promotion and Disease Prevention Objective* Washington, DC: U.S. Department of Health and Human Service Public Health Service, Office of the Assistant Secretary for Healt 1990, pp. 6, 379380. DHHS pub. no. PHS 9150212.

[3] U.S. Department of Health and Human Services. *Healthy Peop 2010: Conference Edition Volumes I and II.* Washington, DC: U Department of Health and Human Services, Public Health Servic Office of the Assistant Secretary for Health, January 2000, pp. 4748.

[4] U.S. Department of Health and Human Services. *Report of the Surgeon General's Workshop on Breastfeeding & Human Lactation.* Rockville, MD: U.S. Department of Health and Human Services, Public Health Service, Health Resources and Services Administration, 1984. DHHS pub. no. HRSDMC 842.

[5] U.S. Department of Health and Human Services. *Followup Report: The Surgeon General's Workshop on Breastfeeding & Human Lactation.* Rockville, MD: U.S. Department of Health and Human Services, Public Health Service, Health Resources and Services Administration, 1985. DHHS pub. no. HRSDMC 852.

[6] Spisak, S, Gross S. *Second Followup Report: The Surgeon General's Workshop on Breastfeeding & Human Lactation.* Washington, DC: National Center for Education in Maternal and Child Health, 1991.

[7] UNICEF/WHO. *Innocenti Declaration on the Protection, Promotion and Support of Breastfeeding.* Florence, Italy: UNICEF and WHO, 1990.

[8] American Academy of Pediatrics. Policy Statement: Breastfeeding and the Use of Human Milk (RE9729). *Pediatrics* 1977;100(6):10351039.

[9] American College of Obstetricians and Gynecologists. *Breastfeeding: Maternal and Infant Aspects.* ACOG Educational Bulletin No. 258. Washington, DC: American College of Obstetricians and Gynecologists, July 2000.

10] American Academy of Family Physicians. *Breastfeeding and Infant Nutrition,* 1994. 1998 1999 AAFP Reference Manual. Washington, DC: American Academy of Family Physicians, 1994, p. 51. http://www.aafp.org/policy/75.html.

11] American Dietetic Association. Position of the American Dietetic Association: Promotion of Breastfeeding. Washington, DC: American Dietetic Association, 1997. *http://www.eatright.org/adap0697.html.*

2] American College of NurseMidwives. Clinical Practices Statement on Breastfeeding. Washington, DC: American College of NurseMidwives, July 27, 1992. *http://www.acnm.org/prof/breast.html.*

3] National Medical Association. *Pediatrics Section of the National Medical Association Statement on Breastfeeding: Promotion, Protection, and Support of Breastfeeding.* Washington, DC: National Medical Association, May 2000.

4] American Public Health Association. *Breastfeeding. APHA Public Policy Statements* No. 7403 (1974), p. 149, and No. 8226 (1982). Washington, DC: American Public Health Association, 1982, p. 308.

[15] U.S. Department of Health and Human Services. *Healthy People 2000: Progress ReviewMaternal and Infant Health.* Hyattsville, MD: U.S. Department of Health and Human Services, Centers for Disease Control and Prevention, National Center for Health Statistics, May 5, 1999, pp. 14. DHHS pub. no. PHS 991256.

[16] U.S. Department of Health and Human Services. *CDC Pediatric Nutrition Surveillance.* Atlanta, GA: U.S. Department of Health and Human Services, Centers for Disease Control and Prevention, 2000.

[17] Caulfield LE, Gross SM, Bentley ME, et al. WICbased interventions to promote breastfeeding among AfricanAmerican women in Baltimore: Effects on breastfeeding initiation and continuation. *J Hum Lact* 1998;14(1):1522.

[18] Beaudry M, Dufour R, Marcoux S. Relation between infant feeding and infections during the first six months of life. *J Pediatr* 1995;126: 191197.

[19] Duncan B, Ey J, Holberg CJ, Wright AL, Martinez FD, Taussig LM. Exclusive breastfeeding for at least 4 months protects against otitis media. *Pediatrics* 1993;91(5):867872.

[20] Frank AL, Taber LH, Glezen WP, Kasel GL, Wells CR, Paredes A Breastfeeding and respiratory virus infection. *Pediatrics* 1982;70(2) 239245.

[21] Howie PW, Forsyth JS, Ogston SA, Clark A, du V Florey C Protective effect of breast feeding against infection. *BM* 1990;300:1116.

[22] Kovar MG, Serdula MK, Marks JS, Fraser DW. Review of th epidemiologic evidence for an association between infant feeding an infant health. *Pediatrics* (Suppl.) 1984;74:S615S638.

[23] Popkin BM, Adair L, Akin JS, Black R, Briscoe J, Fleger, W Breastfeeding and diarrheal morbidity. *Pediatrics* 1990;86(6):874882

[24] Saarinen UM. Prolonged breast feeding as prophylaxis for recurre otitis media. *Acta Paediatric Scandinavia* 1982;71:567571.

[25] Moreland J, Coombs J. Promoting and Supporting Breastfeeding. *A Fam Physician* 2000, 61: 10931100, 21032104.

[26] Ball TM, Wright AL. Health care costs of formula feeding in the fi year of life. *Pediatrics* (Suppl.) 1999;103(4):87076.

[27] Davis MK, Savitz DA, Graubard BI. Infant feeding and childho cancer. *Lancet* 1988;2(8607): 365368.

[28] Davis MK. Review of the evidence for an association between inf feeding and childhood cancer. *Int J Cancer* (Suppl.) 1998;11:2933.

[29] Dewey KG, Heinig MJ, NommsenRivers LA. Differences in morbidity between breastfed and formulafed infants. *J Pediatr* 1995;126(5):696702.

[30] Duffy LC, Byers TE, RiepenhoffTalty M, La Scolea LJ, Zielezny M, Orga PL. The effects of infant feeding on rotavirusinduced gastroenteritis: a prospective study. *Am J Public Health* 1986;76(3):259263.

[31] Heinig MJ, Dewey KG. Health advantages of breast feeding for infants: a critical review. Nutrition Research Reviews 1996;9:89110.

[32] Wright AL, Holberg, CJ, Taussig LM, Martinez, FD. Relationship of infant feeding to recurrent wheezing at age 6 years. *Arch Pediatr Adolesc Med* 1995;149:758763.

[33] Chua S, Arulkumaran S, Lim I, Selamat N, Ratnam SS. Influence of breastfeeding and nipple stimulation on postpartum uterine activity. *Br J Obstet Gynecol* 1994;101:804805.

[34] Dewey KG, Heinig MJ, Nommsen LA. Maternal weightloss patterns during prolonged lactation. *Am J Clin Nutr* 1993;58:162166.

[35] Newcomb PA, Storer BE, Longnecker MP, et al. Lactation and a reduced risk of premenopausal breast cancer. *N Engl J Med* 1994;330(2):8187.

[36] Enger SM, Ross RK, PaganiniHill A, Bernstein L. Breastfeeding experience and breast cancer risk among postmenopausal women. *Cancer Epidemiol Biomarkers Prev* 1998;7(5):365369.

[37] Marcus PM, Baird DD, Millikan RC, Moorman PG, Qaqish B, Newman B. Adolescent reproductive events and subsequent breast cancer risk. *Am J Public Health* 1999;89(8):12441247.

[38] Weiss HA, Potischman NA, Brinton LA, et al. Prenatal and perinatal risk factors for breast cancer in young women. *Epidemiology* 1997;8(2):181187.

[39] Brinton LA, Potischman NA, Swanson CA, et al. Breastfeeding and breast cancer risk. *Cancer Causes and Control* 1995;6:199208.

[40] Newcomb PA, Egan KM, TitusErnstoff L, et al. Lactation in relation to postmenopausal breast cancer. *Am J Epidemiol* 1999;150(2):174182.

[41] Gwinn ML, Lee NC, Rhodes PH, Layde PM, Rubin GL. Pregnancy, breast feeding, and oral contraceptives and the risk of epithelial ovarian cancer. *J Clin Epidemiol* 1990;43(6):559568.

[42] Whittemore AS, Harris R, Itnyre J, and the Collaborative Ovarian Cancer Group. Characteristics relating to ovarian cancer risk: collaborative analysis of 12 US casecontrol studies. II. Invasive

epithelial ovarian cancers in white women. *Am J Epidemiol* 1992;136(10):11841203.

[43] Rosenblatt KA, Thomas DB, and the WHO Collaborative Study of Neoplasia and Steroid Contraceptives. Lactation and the risk of epithelial ovarian cancer. *Int J Epidemiol* 1993;22(2):192 197.

[44] Goldman AS. The immune system of human milk: antimicrobial, antiinflammatory and immunomodulating properties. *Pediatr Infect Dis J* 1993;12(8):664672.

[45] Goldman AS, Goldblum RM, Hanson LA. Antiinflammatory systems in human milk. *Adv Exp Med Biol* 1990;262:6976.

[46] Scariati PD, GrummerStrawn LM, Fein SB. A longitudinal analysis of infant morbidity and the extent of breastfeeding in the United States. *Pediatrics* 1997;99(6):5.

[47] Raisler J, Alexander C, O'Campo P. Breastfeeding and infant illness: a doseresponse relationship? *Am J Public Health* 1999;89(1):2530.

[48] Cushing AH, Samet JM, Lambert WE, et al. Breastfeeding reduces risk of respiratory illness in infants. *Am J Epidemiol* 1998;147(9):863870.

[49] Wright AL, Holbert CJ, Martinez FD, Morgan WJ, Taussig LM, and Group Health Medical Associates. Breast feeding and lower respiratory tract illness in the first year of life. *BMJ* Oct. 14, 1989 299:946949.

[50] Aniansson G, Alm B, Andersson B, et al. A prospective cohort study on breastfeeding and otitis media in Swedish infants. *Pediatr Infec Dis J* 1994;13(3):183188.

[51] Owen MJ, Baldwin CD, Swank PR, Pannu AK, Johnson DL, Howi VM. Relation of infant feeding practices, cigarette smoke exposure and group child care to the onset and duration of otitis media with effusion in the first two years of life. *J Pediatr* 1993;123(5):702711.

[52] Levine OS, Farley M, Harrison LH, at al. Risk factors for invasive pneumococcal disease in children: a populationbased casecontrol study in North America. *Pediatrics* 1999;103(3):28.

[53] Gessner BD, Ussery XT, Parkinson AJ, Breiman RF. Risk factors f invasive disease caused by Streptococcus pneumoniae among Alask native children younger than two years of age. *Pediatr Infect Dis* 1995;14(2):123128.

[54] Pisacane A, Graziano L, Mazzarella G, Scarpellino B, Zona Breastfeeding and urinary tract infection. *J Pediatr* 1992;120(1):878

[55] Marild S, Jodal U, Hanson LA. Breastfeeding and urinarytr infection (letter). *Lancet* 1990;336:942.

[56] Lucas A, Cole TJ. Breast milk and neonatal necrotizing enterocolitis. *Lancet* 1990;336:1519 1523.

[57] Kurscheid T, Holschneider AM. Necrotizing enterocolitis (NEC) mortality and longterm results. *Eur J Pediatr Surg* 1993;3:139143.

[58] Bernt KM, Walker WA. Human milk as a carrier of biochemical messages. *Acta Paediatr* Suppl 1999;430:2741.

[59] Istre GR, Conner JS, Broome CV, Hightower A, Hopkins RS. Risk factors for primary invasive Haemophilus influenzae disease: increased risk from day care attendance and schoolaged household members. *J Pediatr* 1985;106(2):190195.

[60] Cochi SL, Fleming DW, Hightower AW, et al. Primary invasive Haemophilus influenzae type b disease: a populationbased assessment of risk factors. *J Pediatr* 1986;108(6):887896.

[61] Takala AK, Eskola J, Palmgren J, et al. Risk factors of invasive Haemophilus influenzae type b disease among children in Finland. *J Pediatr* 1989;115(5):694701.

[62] HahnZoric M, Fulconis F, Minoli I, et al. Antibody responses to parenteral and oral vaccines are impaired by conventional and low protein formulas as compared to breastfeeding. *Acta Paediatr Scand* 1990;79:11371142.

[63] Pabst HF. Immunomodulation by breastfeeding. *Pediatr Infect Dis J* 1997;16(10):991995.

[64] Garofalo RP, Goldman AS. Expression of functional immunomodulatory and antiinflammatory factors in human milk. *Clin Perinatol* 1999; 26(2):361377.

[65] Nafstad P, Jaakola JJK, Hagen JA, Botten G, Kongerud J. Breastfeeding, maternal smoking and lower respiratory tract infections. *Eur Respir J* 1996;9:26232629.

[66] Picciano MF. Human milk: nutritional aspects of a dynamic food. *Biol Neonate* 1998;74:8493.

[67] Hernell O, Blackberg L. Human milk bile saltstimulated lipase: functional and molecular aspects. *J Pediatr* 1994;125(5)(Pt 2):S56S61.

[68] Dewey KG. Growth characteristics of breastfed compared to formulafed infants. *Biol Neonate* 1998;74:94105.

[69] Meier PP, Brown LP, Hurst NM. Breastfeeding the preterm infant. Chapter 14 In Auerback K, Riordan J. *Breastfeeding*. Gaithersburg, MD: Aspen, 1998, pp. 449480.

[70] Von Kries R, Koletzko B, Sauerwald T, et al. Breast feeding and obesity: cross sectional study. *BMJ* 1999;319:147150.

[71] Ravelli AC, van der Meulen JHP, Osmond C, Barker DJP, Blekes OP. Infant feeding and adult glucose tolerance, lipid profile, blood pressure, and obesity. *Arch Dis Child* 2000;82(3):248252.

[72] Kramer MS. Do breastfeeding and delayed introduction of solid foods protect against subsequent obesity? *J Pediatr* 1981;98(6):883887.

[73] Strbak V, Skultetyova M, Hromadova M, Randuskova A, Macho L. Late effects of breastfeeding and early weaning: sevenyear prospective study in children. *Endocrine Regulation* 1991;25:5357.

[74] Hamosh M. Does infant nutrition affect adiposity and cholesterol levels in the adult? *J Pediatr Gastroenterol Nutr* 1988;7(1):1016.

[75] Elliott KG, Kjolhede CL, Gournis E, Rasmussen KM. Duration of breastfeeding associated with obesity during adolescence. *Obes Res* 1997;5(6):538 541.

[76] Oken E, Lightdale JR. Updates in pediatric nutrition. *Curr Opin Pediatr* 2000;12(3):282290.

[77] Centers for Disease Control and Prevention. *Pediatric Nutrition Surveillance*, 1997 full report. Atlanta: U.S. Department of Health and Human Services, Centers for Disease Control and Prevention, 1998.

[78] PerezBravo F, Carrasco E, GutierrezLopez MD, Martinez MT, Lopez G, Garcia de los Rios M. Genetic predisposition and environmental factors leading to the development of insulindependent diabetes mellitus in Chilean children. *J Mol Med* 1996;74:105109.

[79] Gerstein HC. Cow's milk exposure and type 1 diabetes mellitus. *Diabetes Care* 1994;17(1):1319.

[80] HammondMcKibben D, Dosch HM. Cow's milk, bovine serum albumin, and IDDM: can we settle the controversies? *Diabetes Car* 1997;20(5):897901.

[81] Norris JM, Scott FW. A metaanalysis of infant diet an insulindependent diabetes mellitus: do biases play a role *Epidemiology* 1996;7(1):87 92.

[82] Pettitt DJ, Forman MR, Hanson RL, Knowler, WC, Bonnett PI Breastfeeding and incidence of noninsulindependent diabetes mellit in Pima Indians. *Lancet* 1997;350:166168.

[83] Greco L, Auricchio S, Mayer M, Grimaldi M. Case control study of nutritional risk factors in celiac disease. *J Pediatr Gastro & Nt* 1997;7(3): 395399.

[84] Auricchio S, Follo D, de Ritis, G, et al. Does breast feeding prote against the development of clinical symptoms of celiac disease children? *J Pediatr Gastro & Nutr* 1983(3):2:428433.

[85] FalthMagnusson K, Franzen L, Jansson G, Laurin P, Stenhammar L. Infant feeding history shows distinct differences between Swedish celiac and reference children. *Pediatr Allergy Immunol* 1996;7(3):15.
[86] Ascher H, Krantz I, Rydberg L, Nordin P, Kristiansson B. Influence of infant feeding and gluten intake on celiac disease. *Arch Dis Child* 1997;76:113117.
[87] Ivarsson A, Persson LA, Nystrom L, et al. Epidemic of celiac disease in Swedish children. *Acta Paediatr* 2000;89:165171.
[88] Acheson ED, Truelove SC. Early weaning in the aetiology of ulcerative colitis: a study of feeding in infancy in cases and controls. *BMJ* 1961;2:929933.
[89] Whorwell PJ, Holdstock G, Whorwell GM, Wright R. Bottle feeding, early gastroenteritis, and inflammatory bowel disease. *BMJ* 1979;1:382.
[90] Koletzko S, Sherman P, Corey M, Griffiths A, Smith C. Role of infant feeding practices in development of Crohn's disease in childhood. *BMJ* 1989;298:16171618.
[91] Shu XO, Linet MS, Steinbuch M, et al. Breastfeeding and risk of childhood acute leukemia. *J Natl Cancer Inst.* 1999;91(20):17651772.
[92] Smulevich VB; Solionova LG; Belyakova SV. Parental occupation and other factors and cancer risk in children: I. study methodology and nonoccupational factors. *Int J Cancer* 1999;83:712717.
[93] Gilat T, Hacohen D, Lilos P, Langman MJS. Childhood factors in ulcerative colitis and Crohn's disease: an international cooperative study. *Scand J Gastroenterol* 1987;22:10091024.
[94] Gruber M, Marshall JR, Zielezney M, Lance P. A casecontrol study to examine the influence of maternal perinatal behaviors on the incidence of Crohn's disease. *Gastroenterology Nursing* 1996;19(2):5359.
[95] Rigas A, Rigas B, Glassman M, et al. Breastfeeding and maternal smoking in the etiology of Crohn's disease and ulcerative colitis in childhood. *Ann Epidemiol.* 1993;3(4):387392.
[96] Saarinen UM, Kajosaari M. Breastfeeding as prophylaxis against atopic disease: prospective follow up study until 17 years old. *Lancet* 1995;346:10651069.
[97] Kramer MS. Does breastfeeding help protect against atopic disease? Biology, methodology, and a golden justice of controversy. *J Pediatr* 1988;112(2):181190.
[98] Oddy WH, Holt PG, Sly PD, et al. Association between breast feeding and asthma in 6 year old children: findings of a prospective birth cohort study. *BMJ* 1999;319:815819.

[99] Bjorksten B, Kjellman NIM. Perinatal environmental factors influencing the development of allergy. *Clin Exper Allergy* 1990; 20 Suppl (3):38.

[100] Burr ML, Limb ES, Maguire MJ, et al. Infant feeding, wheezing, and allergy: a prospective study. *Arch Dis Child* 1993;68:724728.

[101] Anderson EW, Johnstone BM, Remax DT. Breastfeeding and cognitive development: a metaanalysis. *A M J Clin Nutr* 1999;70: 525535.

[102] Jacobson SW, Chiodo LM, Jacobson JL. Breastfeeding effects on intelligence quotient in 4 and 11yearold children. *Pediatrics* 1999;103(5):71.

[103] Jensen RG. Lipids in human milk. *Lipids* 1999;34(12):12431271.

[104] Lucas A, Morley R, Cole TJ, Lister G, LeesonPayne C. Breast milk and subsequent intelligence quotient in children born preterm. *Lancet* 1992;339:261264.

[105] Jorgensen MH, Hernell O, Lund P, Holmer G, Michaelsen KF. Visual acuity and erythrocyte docosahexaenoic acid status in breastfed and formulafed term infants during the first four months of life. *Lipids* 1996;31(1):99105.

[106] Richards M, Wadswoth M, RahimiForoushani A, Hardy R, Kuh D, Paul A. Infant nutrition and cognitive development in the first offspring of a national UK birth cohort. *Dev Med Child Neuro* 1998;40:163167.

[107] Hamosh M, Salem N. Longchain polyunsaturated fatty acids. *Bio Neonate* 1998;74:106120.

[108] Heinig MJ, Dewey KG. Health effects of breast feeding for mothers: critical review. *Nutrition Research Reviews* 1997;10:3556.

[109] McNeilly, AS. Lactational amenorrhea. *Endocrinol Metab Clin Nort Am* 1993;22 (1):5973.

[110] Kuzela AL, Stifter CA, Worobey J. Breastfeeding and motherinfa interactions. *J Reprod Infant Psychol* 1990;8:185194.

[111] Windstrom AM, Wahlberg V, Matthiesen AS, et al. Shortterm effec of early suckling and touch of the nipple on maternal behavior. *Ear Hum Dev* 1990;21:153163.

[112] Virden SF. The relationship between infant feeding method a maternal role adjustment. *J NursMidwif* 1988;33(1):3135.

[113] Newcomb PA, Egan KM, TitusErnstoff L, et al. Lactation in relati to postmenopausal breast cancer. *Am J Epidemiol* 1999; 150:174182

[114] Riordan JM. The cost of not breastfeeding: a commentary. *J Hum L* 1997;13(2):9397.

[115] Montgomery DL, Splett PL. Economic benefit of breastfeeding infants enrolled in WIC. *J Am Diet Assoc* 1997;97:379385.
[116] Hoey C, Ware JL. Economic advantages of breastfeeding in an HMO setting: a pilot study. *Am J Man Care* 1997;3(6):861865.
[117] U.S. Department of Commerce. Poverty 1998. Washington, DC: U.S. Department of Commerce, Census Bureau, 1999. *www.census.gov/hhes/poverty.*
[118] Cohen R, Mrtek MB, Mrtek RG. Comparison of maternal absenteeism and infant illness rates among breastfeeding and formulafeeding women in two corporations. *Am J Health Promot* 1995;10(2):148153.
[119] Centers for Disease Control and Prevention. Public Health Service task force recommendations for the use of antiretroviral drugs in pregnant women infected with HIV1 for maternal health and for reducing perinatal HIV1 transmission in the United States. *MMWR* 1998(RR2); 47:130.
[120] American Academy of Pediatrics Committee on Pediatrics AIDS. Evaluation and medical treatment of the HIVexposed infant (RE9721). *Pediatrics* 1997;99(6):909917.
[121] American Academy of Pediatrics Committee on Pediatrics AIDS. Human milk, breastfeeding, and transmission of human immunodeficiency virus in the United States (RE9542). *Pediatrics* 1995; 96(5):977979.
[122] Lawrence, RA. *A review of the medical benefits and contraindications to breastfeeding in the United States.* Maternal and Child Health Technical Information Bulletin. Arlington, VA: National Center for Education in Maternal and Child Health, 1997, pp. 338.
[123] American Academy of Pediatrics Committee on Environmental Health. Chapter 16. Human Milk. In *Handbook of Pediatric Environmental Health.* Elk Grove Village, IL: American Academy of Pediatrics, 1996, pp. 155162.
[124] Rogan WJ. Pollutants in breast milk. *Arch Pediatr Adolesc Med* 1996;150:981990.
[125] Environmental Protection Agency. Update: National Listing of Wildlife Advisories. Washington, DC: Environmental Protection Agency, 1998. *http://www.epa.gov/ost/fish.*
[126] Centers for Disease Control and Prevention. Recommendations for prevention and control of hepatitis C virus (HCV) infection and HCVrelated chronic disease. *MMWR* 1998;47(RR19): 1 39. http://www.cdc.gov/epo/mmwr/preview/mmwrhtm l/00055154.htm.

[127] American Academy of Pediatrics Committee on Drugs. The transfer of drugs and other chemicals into human milk. *Pediatrics* 1994;93(1):137150.

[128] Wilton JM. Breastfeeding and the chemically dependent woman. *NAACOG's Clinical Issues* 1992;3(4):667672.

[129] The Institute of Medicine. *Safety of Silicon Implants*. Washington, DC: National Academy Press, 2000, pp. 248263.

[130] Neal P. Special feeds for special infants 2: feeding the preterm baby. *Prof Care Mother Child* 1995;5(6):151155.

[131] Motzfeldt K, Lilje R, Nylander G. Breastfeeding in phenylketonuria. *Acta Pediatric Suppl*. 1999; 432:2527.

[132] Mennella JA, Beauchamp GK. The transfer of alcohol to human milk. Effects on flavor and the infant's behavior. *N Engl J Med* 1991;325(14): 981985.

[133] Little RE, Anderson KW, Ervin CH, WorthingtonRoberts B, Clarren SK. Maternal alcohol use during breastfeeding and infant mental and motor development at one year. *N Engl J Med* 1989;321(7):425430.

[134] Mennella JA, Beauchamp GK. Smoking and the flavor of breast milk. Letter. *N Engl J Med* 1998;339(21):15591560.

[135] Freed GL, Clark SJ, Sorenson J, Lohr JA, Cefalo R, Curtis P. National assessment of physicians' breastfeeding knowledge, attitudes, training and experience. *JAMA* 1995;273(6):472476.

[136] Freed GL, Clark SJ, Curtis P, Sorenson JR. Breastfeeding educatio and practice in family medicine. *J Fam Pract* 1995;40(3):263269.

[137] Freed GL, Clark SJ, Lohr JA and Sorenson JR. Pediatricia involvement in breastfeeding promotion: a national study of resident and practitioners. *Pediatrics* 1995;96(3):490494.

[138] Freed GL, Clark SJ, Cefalo RC, Sorenson JR. Breastfeeding educatio of obstetricsgynecology residents and practitioners. *Am J Obste Gynecol* 1995;173:16071613.

[139] Schanler RJ, O'Connor KG, Lawrence RA. Pediatricians' practice and attitudes regarding breastfeeding promotion. *Pediatric* 1999;103(3):35.

[140] Dermer A. Overcoming medical and social barriers to breastfeedin *American Family Physician* 1995;51:755763.

[141] Hawthorne K. Intention and reality in infant feeding. *Modern Midwi* 1994;2528.

[142] Gross SM, Caulfield LE, Bentley ME et al. Counseling a motivational videotapes increase duration of breastfeeding

AfricanAmerican WIC participants who initiate breastfeeding. *J Am Diet Assoc* 1998;98(2):143148.
[143] Bentley ME, Caulfied LE, Gross SM, et al. Sources of influence on intention to breastfeed among AfricanAmerican women at entry to WIC. *J Hum Lact* 1999;15(1):2734.
[144] Jolly R. Breastfeeding and health care services. *Int J of Gynecol Ob* 1990;31(S1):79.
[145] PerezEscamilla R, Pollitt E, Lonnerdal B, Dewey KG. Infant feeding policies in maternity wards and their effect on breastfeeding success: an analytical overview. *Am J Public Health* 1994;84(1):8997.
[146] WHO/UNICEF. Protecting, Promoting and Supporting Breastfeeding: The Special Role of Maternity Services. Geneva: World Health Organization, 1989. *http://www.unicef.org/newsline/tenstps.htm.*
[147] World Health Organization. *Evidence for the ten steps to successful breastfeeding.* Geneva: WHO, 1998, pp. 15. Pub No. WHO/CHD 98.9.
[148] UNICEF/WHO. *The UNICEF/Baby Friendly Hospital Initiative: Ten Steps to Successful Breastfeeding.* New York, NY: UNICEF, 1992.
[149] Randolph L, Cooper L, FonsecaBecker F, York M, McIntosh M. *Baby Friendly Hospital Initiative Feasibility Study: Final Report.* Healthy Mothers, Healthy Babies National Coalition Expert Working Group. Internal document. Washington DC: U.S. Department of Health and Human Services, 1994.
[150] U.S. Department of Labor. Women's Jobs: 1964 1999. Washington, DC: U.S. Department of Labor, Women's Bureau, 1999. *http://www2.dol.gov/dol/wb/public/jobs6497.html*
[151] Fein B, Roe B. The effect of work status on initiation and duration of breastfeeding. *Am J Public Health* 1998;88(7):10421046.
[152] Roe B, Whittington LA, Fein SB, Teisl MF. Is there competition between breastfeeding and maternal employment? *Demography* 1999;36(2): 157171.
[153] Bronner YL, Bentley M, Caulfield L, et al. Influence of work or school on breastfeeding among urban WIC participants. *Abstracts of the 124th Annual Meeting of the American Public Health Association.* New York, NY: American Public Health Association,1996.
[154] Gielen AC. Faden RR, O'Campo P, Brown H, Paige, DM. Maternal employment during the early postpartum period: effects on initiation and continuation of breastfeeding. *Pediatrics* 1991;87(3):298305.

[155] HillsBonczyk SG, Avery MD, Savik K, Potter S, Duckett LJ. Women's experiences with combining breastfeeding and employment. *J NurseMidwifery* 1993;38(5):257266.

[156] Bonoan R. *Breastfeeding support at the workplace: best practices to promote health and productivity*. Family Health in Brief. Washington, DC: Washington Business Group on Health, March 2000.

[157] U.S. Department of Health and Human Services. *National Health and Safety Performance Standards: Guidelines for OutofHome Child Care Programs.* Arlington, VA: U.S. Department of Health and Human Services, Health Resources and Services Administration, Maternal and Child Health Bureau, 1992, pp. 117120.

[158] Baranowski T, Bee DE, Rassin DK, et al. Social support, social influence, ethnicity and the breastfeeding decision. *Soc Sci Med* 1983;17(21): 15991611.

[159] Cronenwett LR, Reinhardt R. Support and breastfeeding: a review. *Birth*, 1987; 14:199203.

[160] GrummerStrawn LM, Rice SP, Dugas K, Clark LD, BentonDavis S. An evaluation of breastfeeding promotion through peer counseling in Mississippi WIC clinics. *Maternal and Child Health Journal* 1997;(1)1:3542.

[161] Giugliani ERJ, Caiaffa WT, Vogelhut J, Witter FR, Perman JA. Effect of breastfeeding support from different sources on mothers' decisions to breastfeed. *J Hum Lact* 1994;10(3):157161.

[162] Bronner YL, Kessler L, Gross S, et al. Mother to mother breastfeeding peer counseling: a national WIC survey. *Abstracts of the 122nd Annual Meeting and Exhibition*, American Public Health Association, Public Health and Diversity: Opportunities for Equity. Washington, DC: American Public Health Association, 1994, p. 117.

[163] U.S. Department of Agriculture. Women, Infants, and Children National Breastfeeding Promotion Campaign. *www.fns.usda.gov/wic/content/BF/brpromo/html.*

[164] Giugliani ERJ, Bronner Y, Caiaffa WT, Vogelhurt J, Witter FR, Perman JA. Are fathers prepared to encourage their partners to breastfeed? A study about fathers' knowledge of breastfeeding. *Acta Paediatr* 1994;83:11271131.

[165] Freed Gl, Fraley JK, Schanler RJ. Attitudes of expectant fathers regarding breastfeeding. *Pediatrics* 1992;90(2):224227.

[166] Franklin DL, Wilson, WS. *Ensuring Inequality: The Structural Transformation of the African American Family.* New York, NY: Oxford University Press, Inc, 1997, pp. 1288.

[167] Ekulona E. Family health: taking responsibility/ making the difference. In *The Healthy Start Father's Journal.* Baltimore, MD: Baltimore City Healthy Start, Inc, 1996, pp. 118.

[168] Baumslag N. Breastfeeding, media: lessons learned. In Slussen W, Lange L, Shamez S (Eds). *Report of the National Breastfeeding Policy Conference.* Washington, DC: United States Breastfeeding Committee. UCLA Center for Healthier Children, Families and Communities, 1998, pp. 3739.

[169] Latham MC, Wiessinger MS. Marketing of breastmilk substitutes and obstacles to women's right to breastfeed. In Slussen W, Lange L, Shamez S (Eds). *Report of the National Breastfeeding Policy Conference.* Washington, DC: United States Breastfeeding Committee. UCLA Center for Healthier Children, Families and Communities, 1998, pp. 7380.

[170] Howard C, Howard F, Lawrence R, et al. Office prenatal formula advertising and its effect on breastfeeding patterns. *Obstet Gyneco* 2000;95(2):296303.

[171] Bergevin Y, Doughtry C, Kramer MS. Do infant formula samples shorten the duration of breastfeeding? *Lancet*, 1983;1 (8334):11481151.

[172] Powers NG, Naylor AJ, Wester RA. Hospital policies crucial to breastfeeding success. *Seminars in Perinatology* 1994;18(6):517524.

[173] World Health Organization. *International Code of Marketing of Breastmilk Substitutes.* Geneva: World Health Organization, 1981, pp. 57, 316350.

[174] United States Breastfeeding Committee. *Breastfeeding in the United States: Strategic Plan.* Arlington, VA: U.S. Department of Health and Human Services, Health Resources and Services Administration, Maternal and Child Health Bureau, 2000.

[175] Kleinman RE (Ed). *Pediatric Nutrition Handbook*, 4th Edition. Elk Grove Village, IL: American Academy of Pediatrics, Committee on Nutrition, 1998.

In: Breastfeeding: Laws and Societal Impact ISBN 1-59454-754-8
Editor: Sarah W. Ying, pp. 57-77 

*Chapter 3*

# SUMMARY OF STATE BREASTFEEDING LAWS*

***Douglas Reid Weimer***

## SUMMARY

The practice of breastfeeding has expanded in recent years. Various legal issues have accompanied this development. The primary legal issues concern: 1) the ability of working mothers to breastfeed their children and/or to express milk during working hours; and 2) the nursing and/or expression of milk in public or semi-public places such as restaurants, public transportation facilities, and other locations where the public is present. Certain states have enacted legislation addressing breastfeeding in the workplace and exempting nursing mothers from laws dealing with indecent exposure and/or criminal behavior. Some states have enacted laws that excuse nursing mothers from jury service. State laws vary considerably in their scope and coverage. This report summarizes the various state laws concerning breastfeeding. The current federal legislative proposals concerning breastfeeding are briefly examined in the report.

---

* Excerpted from CRS Report RL31633, dated July 23, 2003.

# INTRODUCTION

One of the stated objectives of the U.S. Public Health Service, as outlined in its report *Healthy People 2010*, is to increase the proportion of mothers who breastfeed their children.[1] The national objective set forth in the report is to strive for a 75% participation rate of nursing mothers in the early postpartum period, a 50% participation rate of nursing mothers in the period after the infant reaches six months of age, and a 25% participation rate of nursing mothers at the age of one year.

Research has indicated that the special composition of human milk enhances cognitive and visual development and lowers the risk and severity of a variety of acute childhood illnesses and chronic diseases, including diarrhea, lower respiratory infection, otitis media, bacteremia, bacterial meningitis, urinary tract infection, necrotizing enterocolitis, lymphoma, and digestive diseases.[2] Research has also demonstrated health benefits to mothers who breastfeed, such as reduced risk of breast and ovarian cancer and osteoporosis.[3]

Because of the growing incidence of women in the workforce, certain issues have arisen concerning working mothers and breastfeeding. It may be necessary for a working mother to express[4] milk during working hours, and/or to breastfeed her child during working hours. Other issues concern the nursing and/or expression of milk in public or semi-public places such as restaurants, public transportation facilities, and other locations where the public is present.

## Development of State Breastfeeding Laws, 1993 to the Present Day

As breastfeeding has become more common, various legal concerns have arisen such as whether certain state decency laws and other laws concerning public nudity and exposure might be inappropriately applied against nursing mothers in public and/or semi-public places. Because of these concerns, a wide range of state laws have been enacted to deal with issues involving various aspects of breastfeeding.

The first state to enact comprehensive breastfeeding legislation was Florida in 1993.[5] This legislation removed breastfeeding from the criminal statutes and created a new law that stated that breastfeeding was an important and basic act of nature that needed to be encouraged in the interests of maternal and child health. The law provided that a woman had a right to breastfeed in any place where she had a right to be. This legislation served as a model for legislation subsequently enacted by other states. In 1994, Florida enacted the first state legislation that examined the importance of breastfeeding mothers having the support and cooperation of their employers when they returned to work.[6] While this law did not require all employers to accommodate nursing mothers (such as providing for a location to lactate), it set out the reasons why breastfeeding was very important. The law also established a study to look at the feasability of breastfeeding guidelines for employers.

Most of the state breastfeeding laws permit mothers to breastfeed in any public or private location and/or provide that breastfeeding does not constitute indecent exposure or other criminal behavior. Some states have vested nursing mothers with certain rights, including rights in the workplace. For example, Hawaii prohibits employers from discriminating against a mother who breastfeeds or expresses milk at the workplace. Other states exempt nursing mothers from jury service. The current body of state breastfeeding laws varies from jurisdiction to jurisdiction. At the current time, thirty-four states have some type of legislation dealing with the protection and/or the promotion of breastfeeding.

## Federal Legislation

Legislation has been introduced in the 108th Congress for the protection of breastfeeding mothers and for the encouragement of breastfeeding. S. 418, the Pregnancy Discrimination Act Amendments of 2003, was introduced by Senator Olympia J. Snowe and would amend the Civil Rights Act of 1964 by adding provisions dealing with breastfeeding. H.R. 2790, the Breastfeeding Promotion Act, was introduced by Representative Carolyn B. Maloney and would amend the Civil Rights Act to protect breastfeeding by new mothers; provide tax incentives for businesses that establish private lactation areas in the workplace; establish a performance standard for breast pumps; and allow breastfeeding equipment to be tax deductible for families.

## Purpose of the Report

The purpose of this report is to summarize the various state laws concerning breastfeeding. Each law is cited and is followed by a brief summary of its provisions. The report does not cover certain commemorative state legislation relating to breastfeeding.[7] A chart has been prepared summarizing the existing state breastfeeding laws and grouping the laws into five categories. Federal legislation introduced in the 108th Congress is summarized.

## SUMMARY OF STATE BREASTFEEDING

### Legislation Alaska

*Alaska Stat. § 01.10.060 (Michie 2000)* provides that in the laws of the state, "lewd conduct," "lewd touching," "immoral conduct," "indecent conduct," and similar terms do not include the act of a woman breastfeeding a child in a public or private location where the woman and child are otherwise authorized to be.

*Alaska Stat. § 29.25.080 (Michie 2000)* provides that breastfeeding does not constitute indecent exposure or other similar offenses in any public or private location. A municipality, borough, or other local government unit cannot implement ordinances banning breastfeeding, or making it a violation of a municipal ordinance.

### California

*Cal. Labor Code § 1030 (West 2002)* requires that employers shall provide break time for an employee to express milk for the employee's infant child. The break time, if possible, is to run concurrently with any break time already provided to an employee.

*Cal. Labor Code § 1031 (West 2002)* requires that an employer make reasonable efforts to provide the employee(s) with a room or a location other than a toilet stall for the employee to express milk in private.

*Cal. Labor Code § 1032 (West 2002)* states that an employer is not required to provide break time if "to do so would seriously disrupt the operations of the employer."

*Cal. Labor Code § 1033 (West 2002)* provides a civil penalty and for the issuance of a citation by the Labor Commissioner. Violations of these provisions relating to breastfeeding are not considered misdemeanors.

*Cal. Civil Proc. Code § 210.5 (West 2002)* permits the mother of a nursing child to postpone jury duty for one year and explicitly eliminates the requirement for the mother to have to appear in person to request the postponement. The one-year period may be extended upon the written request of the mother.

*Cal. Health and Safety Code § 1647 (West 2002)* provides that the procurement, processing, distribution, or use of human milk for human consumption constitutes the rendition of a service.

*Cal. Civil Code § 43.3 (West 2002)* provides the authority for a mother to breastfeed her child in any location.

*Cal. Health and Safety Code §§ 123360, 123365 (West 2002)* mandates the State Department of Health and Human Services to promote breastfeeding in public health campaigns and requires hospitals to provide lactation support and consultation to patients.

*Cal. Assembly Con. Res. 155 (1988)*[8] encourages the state and private employers to support and encourage the practice of breastfeeding by striving to accommodate the need of employees, and by ensuring that employees are provided with adequate facilities for breastfeeding and expressing milk for their children. The governor is authorized to declare by executive order that all state employees be provided with adequate facilities for breastfeeding and expressing milk.

## Connecticut

*Conn. Gen. Stat. Ann. § 31-40w (West 2003)* concerns breastfeeding in the workplace. Employers are required to provide reasonable time and private accommodations each day to an employee who needs to express breast milk for her infant child.

*Conn. Gen. Stat. Ann. §46a-64(a)(3)(West 2002)* forbids resorts and other places of public accommodations from limiting or restricting a mother's right to breastfeed.

*Conn. Gen. Stat. Ann. §53-34b(West 2001)* states that no person may restrict or limit the right of a mother to breastfeed her child.

## Delaware

*Del. Code Ann. tit. 31 § 310 (2002)* provides that a mother is entitled to breastfeed her child in any location of a place of public accommodation wherein the mother is otherwise permitted.

## Florida

*Fla. Stat. Ann. § 383.011 (West 2002)* provides for programs for the encouragement of breastfeeding.

*Fla. Stat. Ann. § 383.015 (West 2002)* permits a mother to breastfeed in any public or private location. A facility may be designated "baby-friendly" if it establishes a breastfeeding policy.

*Fla Stat. Ann. § 383.016 (West 2002)* authorizes the use of a "baby friendly" designation for certain facilities supporting breastfeeding.

*Fla. Stat. Ann. § 383.311 (West 2002)* establishes education and orientation centers dealing with the encouragement of breastfeeding.

*Fla Stat. Ann. § 383.318 (West 2002)* establishes birth centers dealing with instruction in breastfeeding.

*Fla. Stat. Ann. § 800.02 (West 2000)* exempts breastfeeding from the definition of an unnatural and lascivious act.

*Fla. Stat. Ann. § 800.03 (West 2000)* exempts breastfeeding from a statute dealing with the exposure of sexual organs.

*Fla. Stat. Ann. § 800.04(8) (West 2002)* exempts breastfeeding from a statute dealing with lewd or lascivious offenses.

*Fla. Stat. Ann. § 827.071 (West 2002)* provides that a mother's breastfeeding of her baby does not constitute "sexual conduct" within the context of child abuse statutes.

*Fla. Stat. Ann. § 847.001 (West 2002)* provides that a mother' breastfeeding of her baby is not under any circumstance "harmful to minors."

## Georgia

*Ga. Act. No. 922 (S.B. 221)(2002)*[9] provides that the breastfeeding of baby is an important and basic act of nurture which should be encouraged i the interests of maternal and child health. A mother may breastfeed her bab in any location where the mother and baby are otherwise authorized to be. The legislation completely amends existing

Ga. Code Ann. § 31-1-9 (2001). *Ga. Code Ann. § 34-1-6 (2001)* permits employers to provide reasonable, unpaid break time for employees to express breast milk and provides that employers may make reasonable efforts to provide a private location other than a toilet stall for an employee to express milk.

## Hawaii

*Hawaii Rev. Stat. Ann. § 378-2 (Michie 2002)* provides that it shall be an unlawful or discriminatory practice for an employer or labor organization to refuse to hire or discharge from employment, or otherwise penalize a lactating employee because the employee breastfeeds or expresses milk at the workplace.

*Hawaii Rev. Stat. Ann. § 378-10.2 (Michie 2002)* provides that no employer shall prohibit an employee from expressing breastmilk during any meal period or other break period required by law to be provided by the employer or required by a collective bargaining agreement.

*Hawaii Rev. Stat. Ann. §§ 489.21 to 489.23 (Michie 2002)* deals with breastfeeding in places of public accommodation. § 489.21 provides that it is a discriminatory practice to deny or attempt to deny public accommodations to a woman because she is breastfeeding a child. § 489.22 provides that a person injured by an unlawful discriminatory practice may bring a private cause of action and provides appropriate remedies. § 489.23 exempts the provisions dealing with breastfeeding from the purview of the civil rights commission.

## Idaho

*Idaho Code § 2-209 (Michie 1998)* permits a nursing mother to postpone her jury service until she is no longer breastfeeding. “The court shall provide that a mother nursing her child shall have service postponed until she is no longer nursing the child.”

## Illinois

*820 Ill. Comp. Stat. Ann. §§ 260/1; 260/5; 260/10; 260/15; 260/19 (West 2001)* deals with nursing mothers in the workplace. The employer is required to provide reasonable break time and private accommodation (other than a toilet stall) each day to an employee who needs to express breast milk for her infant child.

*20 Ill. Comp. Stat. Ann.§ 2310/2310/442 (West 2001)* allows the State Department of Public Health to conduct an educational breastfeeding public information campaign.

*20 Ill. Comp. Stat. Ann. § 1305/10-25 (West 2002)* provides that the State Department of Human Services may include a program of lactation support services as part of the benefits and services provided for pregnant and breastfeeding participants in the Women, Infants and Children Nutrition Program. The program may include payment for various breastfeeding-related supplies.

*720 Ill. Comp. Stat. Ann. § 5/11-9 (West 2001)* provides that the breastfeeding of a child is not an act of public indecency.

## Indiana

*Ind. Code § 16-35-6 (2003)* allows a woman to breastfeed her child anywhere that the law allows her to be.

## Iowa

*Iowa Code Ann. § 607A.5 (West 2002)* permits a mother who is breastfeeding and who is responsible for the daily care of the child and is not regularly employed to be excused from serving on a jury.

*Iowa Code Ann. § 135.30A (West 2002)* provides that a woman may breastfeed the woman's own child in any public or private location where the mother and the child otherwise are authorized to be present, except the private home or residence of another if the mother's breastfeeding is likely to be viewed by and affront the owner or any occupant of the private home or residence. A mother may breastfeed her child under this section irrespective of whether the nipple of the mother's breast is uncovered during or incidental to the breastfeeding.

## Louisiana

*2002 La. House Concurrent Resolution 35*[10] establishes a joint study concerning the requirement of insurance coverage for outpatient lactation support for new mothers.

*La. Rev. Stat. Ann. 51 § 2247.1 (West 2002)* prohibits discrimination against mothers who breastfeed their babies. Provides that a mother may breastfeed her baby in any place of public accommodation, resort, or amusement, and clarifies that breastfeeding is not a violation of the law.

*2003 La. Acts 369*[11] prohibits any child care facility from discriminating against breastfed babies. Approved by the governor June 18, 2003.

## Maine

*Me. Rev. Stat. Ann. tit. 5, § 4634 (West 2001)* amends the Maine Human Rights Act to declare that a mother has the right to breastfeed her baby in any location, whether public or private, as long as she is otherwise authorized to be in that location.

*Me. Rev. Stat. Ann. tit. 19-a, § 1653 (West 1999)* is intended to protect the health and well-being of a nursing infant of separated or divorcing parents. The law adds the situation of whether the mother is breastfeeding an infant under one year of age to the list of factors that a judge must consider in deciding parental rights and responsibilities.

## Maryland

*Md. Code Ann., Tax-Gen.§ 11-211(b)(19)(2002)* exempts from the sales tax and from the use tax on the sale of tangible personal property that is manufactured for the purpose of initiating, supporting, or sustaining breastfeeding.

*2003 Md. Laws ___ (S.B. 223)*[12] permits a woman to breastfeed her child in any public or private place under specified circumstances and prohibits restrictions on breastfeeding.

## Michigan

*Mich. Comp. Laws Ann. §§ 41.181, 67.1, and 117.4i (West 2002)* excludes a woman breastfeeding a baby, whether or not the nipple or areola is exposed during or incidental to the feeding, from the public nudity laws.

*Mich. Comp. Laws Ann. § 727.27a (West 2002)* concerns child custody. Among the factors to be considered for "parenting time" is whether the child is a nursing child less than six months of age, or less than one year of age if the child receives substantial nutrition through nursing.

## Minnesota

*2000 Minn. Laws Ch. 269*[13] allows a nursing mother, upon request, to be excused from jury service if she is not employed outside of her home and if she is responsible for the daily care of the child.

*Minn. Stat. Ann. § 181.939 (West 2002)* states that an employer must provide reasonable unpaid break time each day to an employee who needs to express breast milk for her infant child. The employer must make reasonable effort to provide a room or other location where the employee can express her milk in privacy and sanitary conditions.

*Minn. Stat. Ann. § 145.905 (West 2002)* provides that a mother may breastfeed in any location, public or private, where the mother and child are otherwise authorized to be, irrespective of whether the nipple of the mother's breast is uncovered during or incidental to the breastfeeding.

## Missouri

*Mo. Ann. Stat. §§ 191.915 and 191.918 (West 2002)* allows mothers to breastfeed, with "appropriate discretion," in any private or public location. Also establishes that all ambulatory surgical centers and hospitals providing obstetrical care are to give new mothers, where appropriate, information on breastfeeding. All obstetrical or gynecological physicians, after January 1, 2000, must give patients information on breastfeeding.

## Montana

*Mont. Code Ann. § 50-19-501 (2002)* provides that the breastfeeding of a child in any location, public or private, cannot be considered a nuisance, indecent exposure, sexual conduct, or obscenity.

## Nevada

*Nev. Rev. Stat. Ann. § 201.210 (Michie 2001)* provides that the breastfeeding of a child by the mother of the child does not constitute an act of open or gross lewdness.

*Nev. Rev. Stat. Ann. § 201.220 (Michie 2001)* provides that the breastfeeding of a child by the mother of the child does not constitute an act of open and indecent or obscene exposure of her body.

*Nev. Rev. Stat. Ann. § 201.232 (Michie 2002)* allows a mother to breastfeed her child in any location where the mother is otherwise authorized to be, irrespective of whether the nipple of the mother's breast is uncovered during or incidental to the breastfeeding.

## New Hampshire

*N.H. Rev. Stat. Ann. § 132:10-d (2002)* states that breastfeeding a child does not constitute an act of indecent exposure. It also notes that restricting or limiting the right of a mother to breastfeed her child is discriminatory.

## New Jersey

*N.J.Rev. Stat. Ann. § 26:4B-4 (2002)* is a law that guarantees a mother the right to breastfeed her baby in any location of a place of public accommodation, resort, or amusement wherein the mother is otherwise permitted. Provides for civil penalties (fines) for violating this law.

## New Mexico

*N.M. Stat. Ann. 28-20-1 (Michie 2002)* states that a mother may breastfeed her child wherever she is authorized to be.

## New York

*N.Y. Civil Rights Law § 79-e (McKinney 2002)* guarantees a mother the right to breastfeed her baby any place she has the right to be, public or private, even if the nipple is exposed during or incidental to breastfeeding.

*N.Y. Corrections Law § 611 (McKinney 2002)* provides that when a woman is committed to a correctional institution and gives birth or is nursing a child in her care under one year of age, the child may accompany/remain with her in the institution.

*N.Y. Penal Law §§ 245.01, 245.02 (McKinney 2002)* exempts breastfeeding from laws governing indecent exposure and from laws prohibiting the promotion of indecent exposure.

## North Carolina

*N.C. Gen. Stat. § 14-190.9 (1999)* states that a breastfeeding mother is not in violation of indecent exposure laws at any time.

## Oregon

*Or. Rev. Stat, § 109.001 (1999)* allows a woman to breastfeed in a public place.

*Or. Rev. Stat. §§ 10.050 (1999)* permits a breastfeeding woman to be excused from acting as a juror, upon the approval of a written request.

## Rhode Island

*R.I. Gen. Laws § 23-72-1 (2001)* guarantees that Department of Health notices on the consumption of fish contaminated with mercury are made available to consumers and explain the dangers to women who expect to be pregnant, are pregnant, or are breastfeeding.

*R.I. Gen. Laws § 11-45-1 (2000)* excludes mothers engaged in breastfeeding from disorderly conduct laws.

## Tennessee

*Tenn. Code Ann. § 50-1-305 (1999)* requires employers to provide reasonable, unpaid break time to an employee to express breast milk and allows employers to provide a room or other private location, other than a toilet stall, for an employee to express breast milk.

## Texas

*Tex. Health & Safety Code Ann. § 161.071 (Vernon 2002)* relates to the provision of donor human milk to certain infants under the medical assistance program.

*Tex. Health & Safety Code Ann. § 165.001 et seq. (Vernon 2001)* authorizes a woman to breastfeed her child in any location and provides for the use of a "motherfriendly" designation for employers who have policies supporting worksite breastfeeding.

## Utah

*Utah Code Ann. § 17-15-25 (1999)* states that city and county governing bodies may not inhibit a woman's right to breastfeed in public. *Utah Code Ann. § 76-10-1229.5 (1999)* states that a breastfeeding woman is not in violation of any obscene or indecent exposure law.

*Utah Code Ann. § 76-9-702 (2002)* provides that a woman's breastfeeding in any location where the woman otherwise may rightfully be, does not under any circumstance constitute a lewd or grossly lewd act, irrespective of whether or not the breast is covered during or incidental to feeding.

*Utah Code Ann. § 10-8-41 (1999)* provides that a woman's breastfeeding, including breastfeeding in any place where the woman otherwise may rightfully be, does not under any circumstance constitute an obscene or lewd act, irrespective of whether or not the breast is covered during or incidental to feeding.

*Utah Code Ann. § 10-8-51 (1999)* provides that a woman's breastfeeding, including breastfeeding in any location where she otherwise may rightfully be, does not under any circumstance constitute a lewd or indecent act, irrespective of whether or not the breast is covered during or incidental to feeding.

## Vermont

*Vt. Stat. Ann. tit. 9, § 4502(j)(2002)* states that breastfeeding a child is an important, basic and natural act of nurture that should be encouraged in the interest of enhancing maternal, child, and family health. The law allows a mother to breastfeed her child in any place of public accommodation in which the mother and child would otherwise have a legal right to be. The law directs the human rights commission to develop and distribute materials and to provide information regarding a woman's legal right to breastfeed her child in a place of public accommodation.

## Virginia

*Va. Code § 2.2-1147.1 (2002)* guarantees a woman the right to breastfeed her child on any property owned, leased, or controlled by the state.

*Va. Code § 18.2-387 (1996)* exempts breastfeeding a child in any public place or place where others are present from indecent exposure statute.

*Va. Joint Resolution # 248 (1994)*[14] requests the Department of Medical Assistance Services to review breastfeeding issues, including lactation education and supplies for Medicaid recipients. Also set forth are the benefits of breastfeeding.

*H.J.Res. 145 (2002)*[15] encourages employers to recognize the benefits of breastfeeding and to provide unpaid break time and appropriate space for employees to breastfeed or express milk.

## Washington

*Wash. Rev. Code Ann. § 9A.88.010 (2002)* provides that the act of breastfeeding or expressing breast milk is not indecent exposure.

*Wash. Rev. Code Ann. § 43.70.640 (West 2002)* exempts breastfeeding from indecent exposure provisions. It also provides for employer/infant friendly promotions relating to work places with facilities conducive to breastfeeding infants.

## Wisconsin

*Wisc. Stat. Ann. §§ 944.17(3), 944.20(2) and 948.10(2) (West 2001)* provides that breastfeeding mothers are not in violation of criminal statutes of indecent or obscene exposure.

## Wyoming

2003 *Wy. H.J.R. 5* [16] (signed by the governor on February 21, 2003) encourages breastfeeding and recognizes the importance of breastfeeding to maternal and child health. The resolution commends public and private employers who provide accommodations for breastfeeding mothers.

## Pending Federal Legislation

In the 108th Congress, two bills have been introduced dealing with breastfeeding, S. 418 and H.R. 2790.

S. 418,[17] the proposed "Pregnancy Discrimination Act Amendments of 2001," was introduced by Senator Olympia J. Snowe on February 14, 2003.[18] The bill would amend Section 701(k) of the Civil Rights Act of 1964[19] by inserting the term "breastfeeding" after the term "childbirth," and by adding at the end, a new section which would state: "In this subsection, the term 'breastfeeding' means the feeding of a child directly from the breast or the expression of milk from the breast by a lactating woman." The practical effect of these amendments would appear to include breastfeeding (including the expression of milk) within the definitions of "because of sex" and "on the basis of sex" for the purposes of the discrimination prohibitions of the Act.

## Comparative Chart of Existing State Breastfeeding Legislation

| States | No Legislation | Mothers permited to breastfeed in any public or private location | Breastfeeding exempted from public indecency laws | Laws relating to breastfeeding in the workplace | Laws exempting breastfeeding mothers from jury duty | Implemented or encouraged development of breastfeeding awareness education campaign |
|---|---|---|---|---|---|---|
| ALABAMA | X | | | | | |
| ALASKA | | | X | | | |
| ARIZONA | X | | | | | |
| ARKANSAS | X | | | | | |
| CALIFORNIA | | X | | X | X | X |
| COLORADO | X | | | | | |
| CONNECTICUT | | X | | X | | |
| DELAWARE | | X | | | | |
| DISTRICT OF COLUMBIA | X | | | | | |
| FLORIDA | | X | X | | | |
| GEORGIA | | X | | X | | |
| HAWAII | | X | | X | | |
| IDAHO | | | | | X | |
| ILLINOIS | | | X | X | | X |
| INDIANA | | X | | | | |
| IOWA | | | | | X | |
| KANSAS | X | | | | | |
| KENTUCKY | X | | | | | |
| LOUISIANA | | X | | | | |

## Comparative Chart of Existing State Breastfeeding Legislation (Continued)

| States | No Legislation | Mothers permitted to breastfeed in any public or private location | Breastfeeding exempted from public indecency laws | Laws relating to breastfeeding in the workplace | Laws exempting breastfeeding mothers from jury duty | Implemented or encouraged development of breastfeeding awareness education campaign |
|---|---|---|---|---|---|---|
| MAINE | | X | | | | |
| MARYLAND | | X | | | | |
| MASSACHUSETTS | X | | | | | |
| MICHIGAN | | | X | | | |
| MINNESOTA | X | | | X | X | |
| MISSISSIPPI | | | | | | |
| MISSOURI | | X | | | | X |
| MONTANA | | | X | | | |
| NEBRASKA | X | | | | | |
| NEVADA | | | X | | | |
| NEW HAMPSHIRE | | | X | | | |
| NEW JERSEY | | X | | | | |
| NEW MEXICO | | X | | | | |
| NEW YORK | | X | | | | |
| NORTH CAROLINA | | X | X | | | |
| NORTH DAKOTA | X | | | | | |
| OHIO | X | | | | | |
| OKLAHOMA | X | | | | | |

## Comparative Chart of Existing State Breastfeeding Legislation (Continued)

| States | No Legislation | Mothers permitted to breastfeed in any public or private location | Breastfeeding exempted from public indecency laws | Laws relating to breastfeeding in the workplace | Laws exempting breastfeeding mothers from jury duty | Implemented or encouraged development of breastfeeding awareness education campaign |
|---|---|---|---|---|---|---|
| OREGON | | X | | | X | |
| PENNSYLVANIA | X | | | | | |
| RHODE ISLAND | | | X | | | |
| SOUTH CAROLINA | X | | | | | |
| SOUTH DAKOTA | X | | | | | |
| TENNESSEE | | | | X | | |
| TEXAS | | X | | X | | |
| UTAH | | | X | | | |
| VERMONT | | X | | | | X |
| VIRGINIA | | X | X | | | |
| WASHINGTON | | | X | X | | |
| WEST VIRGINIA | X | | | | | |
| WISCONSIN | | | X | | | |
| WYOMING–*the breastfeeding law of Wyoming does not fit into any of these categories.* | *See note at left.* | | | | | |

On February 14, 2003, the bill was referred to the Senate Committee on Health, Education, Labor, and Pensions. At the present time, the bill has not emerged from Committee consideration.

H.R. 2790,[20] the proposed "Breastfeeding Promotion Act," was introduced by Representative Carolyn B. Maloney on July 18, 2003.[21] The bill would provide an amendment to the Civil Rights Act of 1964 ("Act") to include lactation (including expression of milk) within the definitions of "because of sex" or "on the basis of sex" for the purposes of the Act. The bill would amend the Internal Revenue Code (IRC) to allow a limited credit to employers for expenses incurred in enabling employed nursing mothers to breastfeed. The bill would also direct the Secretary of Health and Human Services to: 1) put into effect a performance standard for breast pumps irrespective of the class to which the breast pumps have been classified under the Federal Food, Drug, and Cosmetic Act; and 2) issue a compliance policy which would assure that women who want to breastfeed a child are given full and complete information respecting breast pumps. The bill would expand the IRC definition of medical care so as to include qualified breastfeeding equipment and services.

On July 18, 2003, the bill was referred to the House Ways and Means Committee, the House Education and Workforce Committee, and the House Energy and Commerce Committee.

## CONCLUSION

In recent years, there has been an expansion in the practice of breastfeeding. As a consequence of this growing trend, 34 states have enacted legislation associated with breastfeeding. The laws vary considerably in their scope and in their coverage. However, these state laws may be generally classified into five broad categories. Nineteen states permit mothers to breastfeed in any public or private location where the mother is legally entitled to be: California, Connecticut, Delaware, Florida, Georgia, Hawaii, Indiana, Louisiana, Maine, Maryland, Missouri, New Jersey, New Mexico, New York, North Carolina, Oregon, Texas, Vermont, and Virginia. Thirteen states exempt breastfeeding from public indecency laws: Alaska, Florida, Illinois, Michigan, Montana, Nevada, New Hampshire, North Carolina, Rhode Island, Utah, Virginia, Washington, and Wisconsin. Nine states have laws related to breastfeeding in the workplace: California, Connecticut, Georgia, Hawaii, Illinois, Minnesota, Tennessee, Texas, and Washington. Five states exempt breastfeeding mothers from jury duty:

California, Idaho, Iowa, Minnesota, and Oregon. Four states have implemented or encouraged the development of a breastfeeding awareness education campaign: California, Illinois, Missouri, and Vermont.

Federal legislation relating to breastfeeding has been introduced in the 108th Congress. Both S. 418 and H.R. 2790 would amend the Civil Rights Act of 1964 to protect breastfeeding by new mothers. In addition, H.R. 2790 would provide for a performance standard for breast pumps and would provide tax incentives to encourage employers to permit breastfeeding. Neither bill has emerged from Committee consideration at this time.

## REFERENCES

[1] *Healthy People 2010*, Washington, DC: U.S. Department of Health and Human Services, Public Health Service (2000).

[2] *See* American Academy of Pediatrics homepage at [http://www.aap.org/advocacy/bf/ brhist.htm].

[3] *Id.*

[4] A nursing mother "expresses" or extracts breast milk through a vacuum pump device for later feeding to the child.

[5] 1993 Fla. Laws ch. 4, Fla. HB 231. Originally codified at Fla. Stat. § 383.015, §§ 800.02 to 800.04, § 847.001. *See* below for current codification.

[6] 1994 Fla. Laws ch. 217, Fla. SB 1668. Codified at Fla. Stat. §§ 383.011, 383.015, 383.016, 383.311, 383.318.

[7] For example, states may have enacted legislation designating a certain day as "Breastfeeding Day." E.g., Cal. Assembly Con. Res. 95 (1996) proclaimed the week of August 1 through 7, 1996, as "Breastfeeding Awareness Week."

[8] Provision not codified at this time.

[9] To be codified at Ga. Code Ann. § 31-1-9.

[10] Provision not codified at this time.

[11] *Id.*

[12] *Id.*

[13] *Id.*

[14] Apparently, this resolution is not codified in the Virginia Code.

[15] Provision not codified at this time.

[16] *Id.*

[17] 108th Cong., 1st Sess. (2003).

[18] The provisions of S. 418 are substantially similar to the provisions of S. 256, 107th Cong., 1st Sess. (2001). S. 256 was introduced on February 6, 2001, and on the same day was referred to the Senate Health, Education, Labor and Pensions Committee. S. 256 did not emerge from Committee consideration.

[19] 42 U.S.C. § 2000e(k).

[20] 108th Cong., 1st Sess. (2003).

[21] The provisions of the bill are similar to those of H.R. 285, 107th Cong., 1st Sess. (2001) which was introduced by Representative Maloney on January 30, 2001. H.R. 285 did not emerge from Committee consideration.

# INDEX

## C



## D



## E

## J



## K



## L



## M

## N



## O



## P



## R

## Z